KIDS' ATLANTA
From A to Z

Where To Go
What To See
What To Do

Liz White & Jean Feldman

Contributing Writers

Peggy Middendorf, Victoria Schwartz, Martha Jacobs
Susan Palmer, Marnie Goulart, Peggy Milam

Published by:

1991

ACKNOWLEDGEMENTS

Without the help of many people, this book would still be a dream. First of all, to our families, thank you for your patience, support and encouragement. You were the incentive for wanting to create a book of great things for families to do in Atlanta.

A special thanks to Peggy Middendorf for her friendship and invaluable contributions in many areas. The labors of Susan Palmer, Martha Jacobs, Liz Donner, Becky Hire and Jerry Shipp made this book a reality.

Cover illustration: Abby Drue

ISBN 0-9623317-0-8

PREFACE

At the time of printing, all the information in this book was carefully checked. However, organizations move, telephone numbers change, hours fluctuate and prices continue to escalate. Therefore, always call ahead to confirm hours of operation, locations and prices.

NOTE!

The authors do not recommend or endorse any particular program or activity in this book. We do encourage you to visit facilities, ask questions, observe and choose what's best for your family and the ages of your children.

DEDICATION

This book is dedicated to Laura, Holly, Nick and all Atlanta kids. . .

. . .who won't walk down the driveway to pick up the paper but want to run the Peachtree Junior

. . .who hate to take a bath but just love to spend the whole day at White Water

. . .who want a moonwalk, clown, magician and pony rides at their next birthday party

. . .who don't have time for science homework but insist on visiting SciTrek once a month

. . .who will stand in line for hours to ride the "Scream Machine" at Six Flags but can't stand still for 15 minutes in the line at the grocery store

. . .who want to be a ballerina, movie star, baseball player or gymnast when they grow up

. . .whose small hands hold our hearts and love.

Table of Contents

Introduction 1

Attractions 2

Cultural Arts 10

    Art Centers 11

    Dance 13

    Music 16

    Theater 18

    Visual Arts 20

Family Calendar 24

Museums and Historical Sites 49

Parks and Playgrounds 59

Party! Party! Party! 65

Resources and References 75

Science and Nature 84

Shopping 91

Sports and Recreation 98

Tours 113

Trips 119

INTRODUCTION

Atlanta is the Gateway to the South and one of the most exciting cities in the world. The city began as a railroad junction 150 years ago, but now more than 2 million people call Atlanta home. Atlanta is a regional, national and international trend setter in business, economics and transportation. A melting pot of cultures and a kaleidoscope of attractions, entertainment and adventure, the city has many faces—from its labyrinth of expressways and skyscraper lights to green forests and parkland. Its residential areas are among the most beautiful in the country.

KIDS' ATLANTA is a valuable resource for new residents and visitors, as well as a handbook for natives. You'll discover endless possibilities for an action-packed afternoon or a whole year of fun. KIDS' ATLANTA has everything you need from A to Z to plan a party, find a music teacher, learn about mummies or find a special gift. Above all, the book is intended to spark your interest in this wonderful city and to help you build a treasure of memories with your family.

ATTRACTIONS

Whether you want to splash and slide at a huge water park—White Water—or speed up your flow of adrenalin at famous Six Flags Over Georgia, Atlanta's major attractions will occupy you and your family for a day or a whole weekend. Animal lovers will want to head for Zoo Atlanta, but the history buffs will enjoy visiting the Atlanta History Center, the Carter Library or the Martin Luther King Jr. Center for Social Change. Stone Mountain Park offers a combination of amusements aimed at satisfying a variety of tastes, and SciTrek will tickle the young scientist's fancy. Here's a listing of attractions that will appeal to visitors and residents alike.

American Adventures

American Adventures is a family entertainment complex with themes of adventures and turn-of-the century America. It is located adjacent to White Water Park. Offered are indoor and outdoor rides and adventures 365 days a year, including a race track, penny arcade, miniature golf, children's play area, small roller coaster, train ride, carousel, balloon ride and a family restaurant. Most attractions are targeted at children 10 years of age and younger.

250 N. Cobb Parkway   424-9283
Marietta
11 a.m. daily, closing times vary
Pay-as-you-go, 40¢-$1.20 per attraction

Atlanta Botanical Garden

There's always something blooming in Piedmont Park at the Atlanta Botanical Garden. Take the self-guided tour of the herb, vegetable, Japanese, perennial and rose gardens; walk the trails of the 15-acre hardwood forest; then escape to the exotic oasis in the Dorothy Chapman Fuqua Conservatory. There you can view thousands of rare and exotic plants as you travel from an arid desert to a tropical jungle complete with waterfall and birds. There are hands-on projects and educational activities sponsored for children on weekends, as well as many special events, flower shows and exhibits.

1345 Piedmont Ave. N.E.   876-5858
Atlanta
Tuesday-Saturday 9 a.m.-6 p.m., Sunday 12-6 p.m.
Adults, $4.50; children 6-16, $2.25

Atlanta History Center

The Atlanta History Center is a wooded retreat in the middle of Buckhead. The Society complex includes two historic houses, a museum with changing exhibitions, a research library and nature trail. Children enjoy visiting the Tullie Smith House, an 1840s farmhouse complete with a barn and barnyard animals, an herb garden, a vegetable garden, slave cabin and several outbuildings. Rag dolls, old marbles, a spinning wheel and a loom are some of children's favorite antiques in the house.

The Swan House, which was built in 1928 for a wealthy Atlanta family, includes a Victorian playhouse which delights children. Special events, such as the Folk Life Festival in October and the Garden Cavalcade in April, provide opportunities for your child to see pioneer activities, including candle-dipping, blacksmithing, cotton-planting and applesauce-making.

3101 Andrews Dr. N.W.   261-1837
Atlanta
Monday-Saturday 9:30 a.m.-5:30 p.m., Sunday 12 p.m.-5 p.m.
Adults, $6; children 6-17 $3 (no charge Thursday after 1 p.m.)

Carter Presidential Center

On 30 acres overlooking Atlanta's skyline is the Carter Presidential Center. There are films, videos and displays that highlight the presidency itself, as well as Jimmy Carter's administration from 1977-1980. Stroll through the Japanese garden, view gifts and personal memorabilia of the "First Family," visit the model Oval Office and ask Jimmy Carter questions through a unique interactive video. The museum also houses the Task Force for Child Survival, Global 2000 and the Carter Center of Emory University.

One Copenhill Ave. N.E.   331-3942
Atlanta
Monday–Saturday 9 a.m.–4:45 p.m., Sunday 12–4:45 p.m.
Adults, $2.50; children under 16 free

Cyclorama

Next door to the Zoo is the imposing building housing the Cyclorama, a panoramic painting. From its beginnings as a touring panorama, the 400-foot circular canvas depicting the battle of Atlanta has grown into the centerpiece of a museum incorporating a 30-minute film on the campaign to capture the the city; the display of the The Texas locomotive (complete with toy train circling around it); several exhibits on the battles of the Civil War; the soldiers of all ethnic groups who fought in it and their equipment; a video on the restoration of the painting; and touch screen computers that answer questions about the war.

All this may not interest children who have not digested a chapter of Georgia history, but it will entrance Civil War buffs. Seeing the painting itself is a unique experience. A revolving platform enables visitors to view highlights of the battle, and a guide answers questions.

Cherokee Ave., Grant Park   658-7625
Atlanta
9:30 a.m.–5:30 p.m. daily
Adults, $3.50; children 6–12, $2; children under 6, free

Fernbank Science Center and Museum

The DeKalb County Schools' Science Center includes an observatory, museum exhibits, natural science exhibits, a greenhouse, botanical gardens and one of the largest planetariums in the country. Planetarium shows are at 3 p.m. on Wednesday, Friday and Sunday and at 8 p.m., Tuesday through Friday evenings. Be sure and allow plenty of time to visit the exhibit hall, which features moon rocks, the original Apollo space capsule, dinosaurs and much more.

In the 65-acre Fernbank Forest, follow a marked nature trail to learn about the plants and animals of this unique area. And in the greenhouse each month, children are invited to pot a plant and take it home.

The Fernbank Museum, scheduled to open in late 1991, will be the largest natural history museum in the Southeast. It will feature a "Walk Through Time in Georgia," IMAX theater and participatory exhibits.

156 Heaton Park Dr. N.E.   378-4311
Atlanta
Monday 8:30 a.m.–5 p.m., Tuesday–Friday 8:30 a.m.–10 p.m., Saturday 10 a.m.–5 p.m., Sunday 1–5 p.m.
Free Admission
Planetarium shows: Adults, $2; children, $1

Georgia State Capitol

Construction of the Georgia State Capitol began in 1884. The design was Classic Renaissance, and every effort was made to obtain materials from Georgia, such as wood, iron and marble. Even the gold leaf on the shining dome was mined in Georgia.

Take a walk around the Capitol grounds, where you will find a variety of trees, flowers, monuments and markers. Inside and around the rotunda on the main floor is the Hall of Fame with its marble busts and portraits of famous Georgians and Americans. In the south wing, the Hall of States, are flags of the 50 states. The legislative chambers are located on the third floor.

The State Museum of Science and Industry is located on the first and fourth floors. Children are fascinated by the model airplanes, tattered and torn flags, Indian artifacts, a two-headed snake, rocks and minerals. The state wildlife is shown in natural settings.

Tots to grandparents will enjoy a day of browsing at the Capitol. Take MARTA and exit at the Georgia State Station, then stop for lunch or a snack at the Garden Room (across the street from the Capitol on Central Avenue).

Capitol Hill and Washington Street.   656-2844
Atlanta
Monday-Friday 9 a.m.-4 p.m., Saturday 10 a.m.-2 p.m., Sunday 1-3 p.m.
Free admission

High Museum of Art

The High Museum of Art is a six-level, 13,000-square-foot complex that has received international acclaim. The museum exhibits traveling shows and has a permanent collection of paintings, sculpture, prints and decorative arts.

On a trip to the museum with children, the highlight will be "Spectacles," the participatory exhibition on the lower floor. Eight artists have designed spaces that allow children to explore themes on color and light, line and motion, space and shape and illusion. A favorite area is the video room where children's movements are transformed into a myriad of light and color. Other big hits are the felt wall where children can create their own designs and the light table where they can arrange plastic shapes.

1280 Peachtree St. N.E.   892-3600
Atlanta
Tuesday–Saturday 10 a.m.–4:30 p.m., Wednesday 10 a.m.–8:30 p.m., Sunday noon–4:30 p.m.
Adults, $4; students 6–17, $1; children under 6, free (free on Thursday afternoons, 1-5 p.m.)

Lake Lanier Islands

This 1200-acre recreational center is surrounded by 38,000 acres of water. The beach and water park, Wildwaves, includes eight water slide rides, a wavepool, sailboats, paddle boats and miniature golf. There are also stables, rental boats, a challenging golf course, cottages, camping and Lake Lanier Islands Hotel.

GA 365N   1-404-945-6701
Lake Lanier
Parking, $3
Wildwaves, $8.50 per person over 42" tall; $3 under 42"; 2 years and under, free

Martin Luther King Jr. Center

The Martin Luther King Jr. Historic District is a great place to learn about the civil rights leader and Atlanta's black heritage. Dr. King's birthplace, built in 1895, has been restored to its Queen Anne style. Near his home is Ebenezer Baptist Church, where King and his father preached. A memorial park containing the King gravesite with its eternal flame is located between his home and church. Visit Freedom Hall, the educational center, to view a slide presentation of historical events and walk through "Sweet Auburn," the community where many famous blacks resided.

449 Auburn Ave. N.E.   524-1956
Atlanta
10 a.m.–5 p.m. daily
Free admission

The New Georgia Railroad

All aboard! The New Georgia Railroad departs from Zero Mile Post (near Underground Atlanta) and makes an 18-mile circle around Atlanta on most Saturdays. Experience the thrill of riding a train puffed by Old 750—the steam engine that made its maiden run on the Florida East Coast in 1910. The coaches, built in the 1920s, are refurbished with heating and air conditioning to ensure comfort.

The Atlanta loop takes you by landmarks, such as Oakland Cemetery, the Martin Luther King Historic District, Inman Park, Emory University, Peachtree Creek and the Georgia World Congress Center. The trip takes approximately 90 minutes and is narrated by volunteers from the National Railway Historical Society.

On announced dates the train chugs off to Stone Mountain Village. You can browse through the shops and have lunch in the Village, or take MARTA to Stone Mountain Park and catch a later train back to Atlanta. There is also a dinner train to Stone Mountain on weekends to take you back in time to the elegant days of railroad travel.

Georgia Railroad Depot   656-0768 or 656-0769
1 Martin Luther King Jr. Drive
Atlanta
Saturdays 10 a.m., noon and 2 p.m. (call for dates of special excursions)
Adults, $12.50; children 3-12, $5

Kids' Atlanta

SciTrek

The Science and Technology Museum of Atlanta. Turn on your imagination and electrify your mind by touching a magnetic field, defying gravity, freezing your shadow or blowing a gigantic bubble. There's so much to do and learn at the Science and Technology Museum! SciTrek is a "teaching museum" where children and adults learn the basic properties of physical science and the application of these principles through technology. There are separate areas devoted to color, perception, electricity, magnetism and mechanics.

"Kidspace," a special area for young children, is designed for hands-on experiences and family interaction with face painting, keyboards, water play, a construction area and dress-up clothes. There's always something new at SciTrek!

395 Piedmont Ave. N.E.   522-5500
Atlanta
10 a.m.–5 p.m. daily
Adults, $6; children 3–17, $4

Six Flags Over Georgia

Six Flags Over Georgia is a 331-acre theme park that contains more than 100 rides, shows and attractions. For those who like "thrills and chills," try the Z-Force roller coaster, the Mind Bender (triple-loop roller coaster), the Cyclone and Free Fall. To cool off, take a plunge on the log ride, Thunder River, or Splashwater Falls. For the younger set there is Looney Tunes Land with a play fort, scaled down rides and an old-fashioned carousel. The whole family will enjoy the Dolphin Show, Crystal Pistol Show, Bugs Bunny Show and other entertainment throughout the park.

Six Flags Road at I-20   739-3400
Austell
10 a.m. daily in the summer (closing times vary); open weekends in the spring and fall
Adults, $20; chilldren under 48 inches, $10; children under 3, free
(Season and family passes available)

Stone Mountain Park

Stone Mountain Park is the 3,200-acre home of the world's largest mass of exposed granite and a huge carving. The carving is a memorial to Confederate War heroes Robert E. Lee, Stonewall Jackson and Jefferson Davis. Other attractions include an ice rink, skylift, antebellum mansion, steam-driven locomotive, riverboat, antique auto and music museum, game ranch (with petting area), Civil War exhibits, hiking, tennis, golf, fishing, camping, an inn and restaurants.

A favorite summer activity at the park is Waterworks (beach area, water slides, mini golf). Another popular summer activity is the Lasershow, which is presented nightly after sundown. Laser beams project cartoons, stories and graphic images on the mountain, all choreographed to jazz, popular and classical music. Any time of year it's fun to take the 1-mile hike up and down the mountain.

Stone Mountain (exit off U.S. 78)   498-5600
Stone Mountain
6 a.m.–midnight daily
(Attractions operate from 10 a.m.–5:30 p.m., later in summer)
$20 annual vehicle parking permit, $5 daily permit
Most attractions are $2.50 adults; $1.50 children 3–11

Underground Atlanta

The 138-foot light tower of Underground marks the spot where Atlanta took root. It's "the place to be in Atlanta" with history, local color and fun for all ages. The six city blocks and 12 acres of Underground boast 20 spectacular restaurants, more than 100 specialty shops, streetcar merchants and exciting entertainment. The entry plaza features cascading water fountains and an amphitheater where live performances are held. Board the New Georgia Railroad, see the World of Coca-Cola Pavilion and visit Atlanta Heritage Row. Underground Atlanta is truly a unique blend of the old and new and is a gathering place for residents as well as visitors.

Peachtree Street at Alabama Street   523-2311
Atlanta
10 a.m. - till the wee hours
Free admission

White Water Park

This 35-acre water park has raft rides, speed rides, body flumes, a wave pool and a children's section (Little Squirt's Island). If you want to relax, grab a tube and float down the Suwannee River or Little Hooch. Maybe you'd like to try the Atlanta Ocean with its 4-foot waves for rafting and body surfing. For more excitement, there's the Caribbean Plunge, the Dragon's Tail Falls, the White Water Rapids and the Tidal Wave.

Little Squirt's Island offers more than 25 activities for children under 48 inches tall. In this shallow children's pool, there are miniature slides, a tame inner tube ride, a Playport, water cannons, squirt guns and a mushroom waterfall. And in all parts of the park are certified lifeguards and life jackets for non-swimmers.

250 N. Cobb Parkway N.E.   424-9283
Marietta
10 a.m. from Memorial Day through the first weekend in September (closing times vary)
Adults, $14.99; children under 48 inches tall, $8.99; children under 4 and seniors 62 and older, free.

Kevin Sartain

Zoo Atlanta

Zoo Atlanta

Zoo Atlanta is home for nearly 1,000 animals (250 species), including black rhinos, Chilean flamingos, sea lions, polar bears, Vietnamese pot-bellied pigs, small monkeys, elephants, waterfowl, an assortment of birds, and one of the largest reptile collections in the country. The five-acre Ford African Rain Forest is occupied by three family groups of gorillas, of which the most famous is Willie B. And don't miss the Masai Mara exhibit of the savannas of East Africa, with giraffes, lions and zebras. There are also shows in the Wildlife Theater, including "The Greatest Baby Elephant Show on Earth," animals to pet and feed in the Children's Zoo and a miniature train to ride.

Grant Park   624-5678
800 Cherokee Ave. S.E.
Atlanta
10 a.m.-5 p.m. daily
Adults, $6.75; children 3-11, $4; children under 3, free

CULTURAL ARTS

Ballet Rotaru

A tlanta is alive with art, dance, music and theater. In addition to the Atlanta Ballet, the Atlanta Symphony Orchestra and legitimate theater at the Atlanta Arts Alliance, a host of performances are offered by small repertory companies, semi-professional groups and churches. Whether they are interested in puppet shows or holiday pageants, your family will be able to attend spectacular productions throughout the year. The city is rich in visual arts as well, with galleries and permanent museum collections displaying everything from photographs to paintings. This section highlights both the performing and visual arts, and it includes a listing of opportunities for children to develop their own talents in these areas. Here in Atlanta, an abundance of art classes, music classes, drama classes and more are readily available to your budding artist or actor.

Art Centers

It is our responsibility as parents to nurture an appreciation for many forms of art in our children. These comprehensive art centers offer exhibits, performances and classes for each member of the family.

A.R.T. Station. Located in Stone Mountain, A.R.T. Station is a non-profit professional art center. There are exhibits in the gallery that change every two months as well as theatrical performances, concerts and dance productions. Art classes are available for children through adults in visual, literary and performing arts.

985 Third Street   469-1105
Stone Mountain

Callanwolde Fine Arts Center. Located in the 1920s mansion of former Coca-Cola president Charles Howard Candler, Callanwolde is an outstanding cultural and arts facility. The mansion and grounds feature nature trails, a rock garden, stained glass and bronze balustrades. The house features an Aeolian organ that has 3,752 pipes, the largest of its kind in working condition. Outlets from the tone chamber reach every room in the house. The Callanwolde Concert Band, Callanwolde Poetry Committee, The Young Singers of Callanwolde and the Southern Order of Storytellers perform on a regular basis. There is an art gallery, pottery studio and photography lab. Lectures, classes and exhibits are offered throughout the year.

980 Briarcliff Road N.E.   872-5338
Atlanta

Mable Cultural Center. Sponsored by the South Cobb Arts Alliance, Mable House hosts guest artists in monthly exhibits. Classes in all the arts are offered for children and adults. Also, a 'Candlelite Concert' series takes place during the summer months.

5239 Floyd Road   739-0189
Mableton

Marietta/Cobb Museum of Art. Now with a permanent collection, the exhibits in their three galleries change frequently. The educational programs relate to the current exhibit or permanent collection. Located in the old Post Office and Cobb Central Library, the museum is in an appropriate setting.

30 Atlanta Street   424-8142
Marietta

North Arts Center. Exhibits change frequently in the 7,000-square-foot gallery. They also offer a performing arts series featuring drama and music. More than 150 classes are offered each quarter for children through adults in visual, performing and literary arts.

5339 Chamblee Dunwoody Road 394-3447
Dunwoody

Steeplehouse Arts Center. Associated with Cobb Parks and Recreation, the Steeplehouse Arts Center features monthly gallery exhibits. Art classes are available in all the different arts and include classes for preschoolers through adult, including family classes.

300 Village Place 952-8661
Marietta

Soapstone Center for the Arts. Different artists are featured in monthly exhibits. Soapstone also showcases various artists at South DeKalb Mall. Classes are available in visual and performing arts as well as arts and crafts.

2853 Candler Road 241-2453
Decatur

Dance Fashions

Dance

Shall we dance? Atlanta has a rich resource of talented dancers dedicated to performing, as well as teaching children of all ages and at all levels.

Atlanta Ballet. The Atlanta Ballet repertory company is the oldest continually performing ballet company in the United States. During the Christmas season, they perform "The Nutcracker Suite" at the Fox Theatre and the dancing, costumes, sets and music never fail to delight audiences of all ages.

Atlanta Ballet Company   873-5811
477 Peachtree Street N.E.
Atlanta

Ballet Rotaru Pavel Rotaru launched his ballet company in 1988. Ballets from the classical repertoire are performed four times a year at the Fox Theatre.

721 Miami Circle   266-8500
Atlanta

Carl Ratcliff Dance Theatre. This modern dance troupe is most active in spring and fall.

726 Mill Walk N.W.   266-0010
Atlanta

Classes in many dance disciplines are available throughout the city:

A Blaze Company in Motion. Ballet, tap, jazz and acrobatics for ages 3 years through adult.

790 Indian Trail Road   925-2222
Lilburn

Atlanta Dance Centre. Ballet, tap and jazz for children and adults.

Decatur and College Park   761-2698

Atlanta School of Ballet. The official school of the Atlanta Ballet Company, the Atlanta School of Ballet offers classical ballet training.

3215 Cains Hill Place N.W.   874-8695
Atlanta

Barbara Bramble Dancecenter and Dance Atlanta. Established in 1964, the Dancecenter offers classes in ballet, tap, jazz and teaches talent show routines.

5270 Peachtree Parkway   448-5437
Norcross

Carol Walker Southern Dance Academy. Established in 1969, co-ed classes in ballet, tap, jazz and creative movement are avilable for preschoolers through adult.

420 North Indian Creek Drive   292-3700
Clarkston

Dan & Company Studio. The official school of "Atlanta Jazz Theatre" offers lessons in ballet, tap, drama and voice.

5544 Chamblee Dunwoody Road   393-9519
Dunwoody

4880 Lower Roswell Road N.E.   971-1681
Marietta

Dance and Arts Showcase. Offers ballet, tap, jazz, creative movement and baton classes for ages 2 through adult.

Doraville and Lawrenceville   457-3173

Dance Arts Centre. Offers classes in ballet, tap, jazz, acrobatics and pre-dance.

2856 Buford Highway   476-3054
Duluth

Dance Mania. Ballet, jazz, tap and combination classes available for ages 3 through adult.

595 E. Crossville Road   594-0650
Roswell

Dance Stop. Classes for beginner to professional in ballet, jazz, tap, modern and drama.

1547 Roswell Road   971-1109
Marietta

1401 Johnson Ferry Road   578-0048
Marietta

3162 Johnson Ferry Road   640-7702
Marietta

Dancer's Studio. Ballet, pointe, jazz and tap classes and home of Atlanta Dance Unlimited.

Beaver Ruin Road   662-8144
Norcross

3658 Shallowford Road   993-2623
Doraville

Decatur School of Ballet. Established in 1947, the Decatur School of Ballet teaches classical ballet as well as jazz, modern dance and ballroom.

102 Church Street   378-3388
Decatur

Dolores Werner Performing Arts Studio. Graded classes for ballet, tap, jazz, acrobatics, adagio and dance-r-size.

4445 Hugh Howell Road   939-2787
Tucker

1025 Killian Hill Road   923-1314
Lilburn

Doris Russell School of Performing Arts. Classes for children ages 4 through 12 in creative movement, ballet, tap, jazz, theater arts and more.

274 Senoia Road   964-5057
Fairburn

Druid Hills Dance Centre. Ballet and jazz classes for children through adult.

2949 N. Druid Hills Road N.E.   633-2144
Atlanta

Duluth School of Ballet. Ballet, pointe, jazz and early childhood program for ages 3 through adult.

3131 S. Peachtree Street   476-4306
Duluth

En Pointe School of Dance. Classes for ages 3 and up in creative movement, ballet, jazz and tap.

5334 Highway 29   381-5787
Lilburn

First Step. Classes for ages 3 and up in dance, creative movement, pre-gym, drama and music.

634-0554

Fleetwood Studios. The Fleetwood Studios offer classes in ballet, tap and jazz and have a resident performing company. Ages 3 through college.

2791 Clairmont Road N.E.   633-6619
Atlanta

Footsteps Dance Studios. Pre-tap, pre-ballet, creative movement, jazz, ballet and tap for school-age children through adults.

2151 Godby Road   997-9383
College Park

Georgia Baton and Dance Studio. Tap, ballet, jazz, baton, acrobatics and pre-ballet for all ages.

4245 Walking Lane   921-2658
Lilburn

Gwinnett Dance Academy. Ballet, jazz, tap, creative movement and ballroom for ages 3 and up.

4814 Highway 78   985-1290
Lilburn

Lee Harper & Dancers Studio Inc. Creative movement, pre-ballet, ballet, modern dance, jazz, musical theater, tap and dance for cheerleaders as well as the home of DancerKids, a junior company.

721 Miami Circle N.E.   261-7416
Atlanta

Rotaru Ballet School. Kirov training.

721 Miami Circle   266-8566
Atlanta

Ruth Mitchell Dance Studio. Classical, ballet, jazz and tap are available to the beginner through professional at Ruth Mitchell Dance Studio. Established in 1956.

3509 Northside Parkway N.W.   237-8829
Atlanta

Susan Chambers Studio of Theatre Dance. Classes for ages 3 through adult in creative movement, tap, ballet, jazz and drama.

166 E. Crogan Street   962-0195
Lawrenceville

Tolbert Yilmaz School of Dance, Inc. Ballet, pointe, jazz, tap, gymnastics and baton for beginners through professional.

1217 Canton Street   998-0259
Roswell

Music

Musical opportunities abound for children in Atlanta from performances to lessons. Tap into children's natural interest in music by attending concerts and performances presented by the following groups:

Atlanta Opera. The Atlanta Opera offers three selections each year, performed at Symphony Hall.

1800 Peachtree Street N.E.   355-3311
Atlanta

Atlanta Symphony Orchestra. The Atlanta Symphony Orchestra is housed in the Woodruff Arts Center. The Symphony enables Atlantans of all ages to enjoy magnificent music. In addition to the regular subscription series of concerts, the Symphony offers a family concert series on three Saturday mornings during the year. Also, a free summer concert series at area parks allows even young children to enjoy the Symphony with a picnic followed by the evening stars.

Robert W. Woodruff Arts Center   898-1182
1280 Peachtree Street N.E.
Atlanta

Cobb Symphony Orchestra. This community orchestra performs four concerts a year plus a family holiday concert.

Jennie T. Anderson Theater   424-5541
Cobb Civic Center
548 Clay Street
Marietta

DeKalb Symphony Orchestra. Sponsored by DeKalb Community College, the DeKalb Symphony Orchestra presents a year-round series of concerts and recitals by students and guest performers.

Division of Fine Arts   299-4136
DeKalb Community College
555 N. Indian Creek Drive
Clarkston

Auditions

Children will enjoy singing with their local church or school choir, or they may want to audition for one of the choral groups listed below:

The Atlanta Boy Choir Inc. The Atlanta Boy Choir performs throughout Europe and the United States. In Atlanta, the choir holds annual Christmas and spring concerts. Auditions are three times a year: in September, January and April.

1215 S. Ponce de Leon Ave. N.E.   378-0064
Atlanta

Atlanta's Children's Chorale. Program includes music and vocal training, musical movement, songs in foreign language, ensemble singing and concerts for boys and girls from kindergarten to fifth grade.

North Buckhead/Sandy Springs   728-0643

Atlanta Music Club. The Atlanta Music Club is Atlanta's oldest, chartered, non-profit music organization. The club sponsors the Young Performers of Atlanta, featuring talented students from the third to twelfth grade.

1900 The Exchange   955-5416
Suite 160
Atlanta

The Atlanta Symphony Youth Orchestra. Composed of high school students, the Atlanta Symphony Youth Orchestra performs several times a year at Symphony Hall. Students must be at least 14 years old and members of a school music program to audition for a place in the orchestra. Auditions are in September.

Robert W. Woodruff Arts Center   898-1177
1280 Peachtree Street N.E.
Atlanta

Cobb Youth Chorale. Music theory is emphasized in the Cobb Youth Chorale training program. First through eight graders may apply to join the group. The Chorale performs several times each year and tours annually.

Box 316   425-2271
Marietta, 30061

Young Singers of Callanwolde. Children ages 8 through 14 can try out for the Young Singers of Callanwolde. Auditions are in April.

315 W. Ponce de Leon Ave.   377-6081
Decatur

DeKalb Youth Symphony. This group meets after school at Lakeside High School.
3801 Briarcliff Road N.E.   633-2631
Atlanta

Music Lessons

Music instruction is available through private teachers, group lessons and music stores. These businesses specialize in children's lessons.

Atlanta Music Center. Since 1975, the Atlanta Music Center has taught children ages 3 and up using the Yamaha and Suzuki methods. In addition to group lessons, private instruction is offered in all instruments and voice.
Dunwoody Village   394-1727
Lilburn/Stone Mountain   979-2887
E. Cobb   977-0003

Georgia Academy of Music. Classes for children and adults are offered at the Georgia Academy of Music, including violin and cello for the very young, a children's ensemble, a Mozart ensemble, an adult cello choir and a music theory class.
P.O. Box 250347   355-3451
Atlanta 30325

Classes: 1424 W. Paces Ferry Road N.W., Atlanta

Kindermusik of Atlanta. Taught in the U.S. since 1978, Kindermusik is the English-language adaptation of the program developed by the Association of West German Music Schools. Creative movement, music improvisation, ear training and experimentation with orchestral instruments are all incorporated into the program. Kindermusik is taught in eight locations in the Atlanta area.

449-0837

Make Music! Music and movement program based on Dalcroze Eurhythmics and Orf techniques. Classes are offered for children ages 6 months through 8 years.

Marietta   565-6392

Musicare Inc. Musicare operates in childcare centers throughout metro Atlanta. Musicare teachers use puppets, rhythm instruments, the glockenspiel and movement equipment to teach basic musical concepts.

Musicare Inc.   476-5208

Theater

"All of the world's a stage," and children are always delighted with live performances. Many theatrical companies in Atlanta occasionally present a children's show or produce a show that uses children in the cast. Upcoming auditions are announced in the Saturday entertainment section of the daily paper.

Alliance Theatre. One of the nation's largest theaters, the Alliance was established in 1968. The 800-seat mainstage proscenium theater has been the setting for an impressive list of productions from Shakespeare to current Broadway and off-Broadway plays.

Robert W. Woodruff Arts Center
1280 Peachtree St. N.E.   892-2414
Atlanta

Alliance Children's Theatre. Established in the late 1920s as the Atlanta Children's Theatre, the Theatre was originally a project of the Junior League. The Alliance Children's Theatre has been a full professional company since 1968. The company performs adaptations of classics and original works for children on the Alliance mainstage and also tours throughout the country and in-state.

Robert W. Woodruff Arts Center
1280 Peachtree St. N.E.   898-1128
Atlanta

Center for Puppetry Arts. The most comprehensive puppetry center in the nation, the Center for Puppetry Arts is a very special place. Performances for children, and anyone who has ever loved a puppet, run year-round. The center offers classes in puppetry and workshops on how to make puppets. The museum contains the largest private collection of puppets in America. One exhibit traces the history of puppetry and the art of puppet making, with figures from around the world.

1404 Spring St. N.W.   873-3391
Atlanta

Fox Theatre. Built as a movie palace in the 1920s, the Fox Theatre is listed with the National Register of Historic Places. The Fox Theatre is a wonderful setting for performances of Broadway plays and musical talent. The theater boasts a majestic original period organ and sing-alongs take place prior to movies shown in the summer.

660 Peachtree St. N.E.   881-2000
Atlanta

Georgia Shakespeare Festival. The most famous playwright in the world is represented by the Georgia Shakespeare Festival, and in the summer, children ages 5-12 can attend a two hour "Camp Shakespeare" workshop.

Oglethorpe University   233-1717
Atlanta

Theatre of the Stars. Broadway musicals are popular at Theater of the Stars. Everyone gets dressed up and excitement fills the air.

4469 Stella Drive N.E.   252-8960
Atlanta

Drama Lessons

Children are natural actors and actresses, and their dramatic abilities can be encouraged at one of the following facilities:

Alliance Theatre School. Part of the Alliance Theatre Company, the Alliance Theatre School offers classes for children of all ages.

Robert W. Woodruff Arts Center
1280 Peachtree Street N.E.   898-1131
Atlanta

Atlanta Workshop Players. Offers acting classes, improvisation, mime, on-camera commercial and film acting and audition techniques.

951-1956

Cobb Childrens Theater. This production company offers two performances each year using middle and high school students.

5195 Clark Street S.W.   941-1391
Austell

Alliance Theatre School

Doraville Arts Theater. Children through adults can sign up for acting, singing and dancing lessons.

Doraville Recreation Center   451-0573
3765 Park Ave.
Doraville

DramaArt School of Drama. As part of Art/Play, the School of Drama provides classes for children ages 3½ through teens. The school emphasizes development of the children's personal style. Classes are offered year-round and students have the opportunity to perform original works written by staff members.

Rio Shopping Center   984-8914
595 Piedmont Ave. N.E.
Atlanta

Dunwoody Stage Door Players. Acting and performance classes for children ages 6-17 include theater games, improvisation, story play and stage techniques.

396-1726

Visual Arts

Children are fascinated by visual arts, whether it's a priceless Renaissance sculpture or their latest finger painting. Exposing them to the array of visual arts that Atlanta has to offer will expand their horizons and allow them to appreciate all forms of art. And if your Rembrandt is really inspired, you may want to invest in some children's art lessons.

High Museum of Art. The modern, white-tiled building is well-known nationally for its design, and collections and special exhibits within. A four-story atrium is the centerpiece of the museum and interlocking galleries contain American, European, Modern and African art, American decorative arts, European porcelain and a variety of prestigious traveling exhibitions. "Spectacles," a Junior Gallery exhibit for children, is a participatory exhibit providing an opportunity to experience different aspects of art such as line, color, perspective and texture. There is also an activities area featuring a velcro art wall.

1280 Peachtree St. N.E.   892-3600
Atlanta

Art Lessons

The "young at art" can take lessons and develop their creative abilities at one of the following locations:

Academy Art Gallery and Studio
962-3078
128 E. Crogan Street
Lawrenceville

A.R.T. Station
469-1105
985 Third Street
Stone Mountain

Atlanta College of Art
898-1169
1280 Peachtree Street N.E.
Atlanta

Chastain Arts Center
424-8142
30 Atlanta Street N.E.
Marietta

Galloway Center for the Arts
252-8389
215 W. Wieuca Road N.W.
Atlanta

Pinckneyville Arts Center
449-5910
4300 Holcomb Bridge Road
Norcross

Art in Public Places

It is easy to forget art while driving around, but the city has filled many public places with art. Following is only a small sample of the fine art found in public spaces. Go out one day and discover public art.

At **Hartsfield Airport** you will see serial works by artists on your way from the gate to baggage claim. Six of the MARTA stations include murals, mosaics and sculptures. At the intersection of Spring and Carnegie Way there is a bronze sculpture by Mark Smith, titled *Emerging*. At **Piedmont Park** a sculptured playground, "Playscapes," was done by Isamu Noguchi. And John Feight has brought a beautiful, loving touch to many Atlanta hospitals, including **Northside** and **Scottish Rite Hospital**. This man paints murals on hospital walls—creating seascapes, jungle landscapes and other designs to bring a smile to the sick. His work is now in some Russian hospitals.

Galleries

There are many unique and professional galleries in Atlanta. Most of them are grouped in three areas of the city—downtown, midtown and Buckhead. Spending an afternoon browsing galleries can be a pleasurable way for children to see fine art. Here is just a sampling of the galleries in Atlanta.

Abstein Gallery. The Abstein Gallery displays original art by Atlanta and regional artists with a wide range of styles from traditional to eclectic.

558 14th St. N.W.   872-8020
Atlanta

Atlanta Art Gallery. The Atlanta Art Gallery specializes in American and European paintings of the last two centuries.

262 E. Paces Ferry Road N.E.　261-1233
Buckhead

Carlson & Lobrano Galleries Ltd. Everything from evolving art in the Southeast to signed original *New Yorker* cartoons can be found at Carlson & Lobrano Galleries. Five house artists do original works on commission.

55 Bennett St. N.W.　351-9897
Atlanta

Frabel Gallery. Features the original and signed crystal sculptures of Hans Frabel.

Peachtree Center Gallery　659-2832
Peachtree Center
Atlanta

Georgia State University Gallery. Changing exhibits of nationally known artists and students are shown at Georgia State University Gallery.

Art and Music Building　658-2257
10 Ivy St.
Atlanta

Center for Puppetry Arts

Goethe Institute. The German cultural center has changing exhibits of German art.

400 Colony Square N.E.   892-2388
Midtown
Atlanta

TULA Showrooms & Studios. Since 1974, TULA has showcased a new approach to art. TULA houses both galleries and artists' studios, allowing visitors a chance to see both works in progress and finished pieces.

75 Bennett St. N.W.   351-3551
Atlanta

FAMILY CALENDAR

A tlanta has a rich offering of annual events that are geared toward the family. School carnivals. . .neighborhood ice cream socials...country fairs...arts festivals. There's something going on in Atlanta every month to provide entertainment, food and fun for both visitors and residents. The Children's Festival in February, the Dogwood Festival in the spring, free symphony concerts in the parks throughout the summer, the Arts Festival in Piedmont Park in the fall and the Festival of Trees in December are but a few of the many events that families look forward to each year. Pencil these in on your calendar now, but be sure to check Atlanta Parent newspaper or the Atlanta Journal-Constitution for up-to-date information at the time of the event.

January

Children's Concert. The DeKalb Symphony Orchestra Children's Concert introduces children of all ages to the sounds of a symphony orchestra.
DeKalb College Gymnasium   299-4136
555 N. Indian Creek Drive
Clarkston

Harlem Globetrotters. The whole family, even non-sporting members, will enjoy the world-class ball handling and sharp shooting combined with the comedy of the Harlem Globetrotters basketball team in this action-packed performance.
Omni   681-6400
100 Techwood Drive N.W.
Atlanta

Magic of David Copperfield. Magic and illusions to astound the family, incorporating music, choreography and storylines, appeal to every age.
Fox Theatre   881-2100
660 Peachtree St. N.E.
Atlanta

Martin Luther King Jr. Annual Parade. Floats, bands and marching units are all part of the festivities celebrating Martin Luther King Jr.'s birthday. College and high school bands and marching units from across the Southeast perform. Parade ends at the King Center.
Martin Luther King Jr. Center   524-1956
449 Auburn Ave. N.E.
Atlanta

Olde Christmas Storytelling Festival. Storytellers from throughout the Southeast gather to entertain festival-goers with stories, music, dancing and workshops for both children and parents.
Callanwolde   872-5338
980 Briarcliff Road, N.E.
Atlanta

Ringling Bros. and Barnum & Bailey Circus. "The Greatest Show on Earth" is presented in the classic three-ring circus and includes trapeze acts, acrobats, riders, animal acts and more.
Omni   681-2100
100 Techwood Drive N.W.
Atlanta

Summer Expo. Summer programs, camps and activities targeted for youths ages 12 and up. Children and parents meet representatives from local, national and international summer programs.

Westminster Schools   355-8673
1424 West Paces Ferry Road N.W.
Atlanta

February

Atlanta Flower Show. Experience a breath of springtime in the winter. Thousands of flowers in early bloom in many different landscaped gardens. A must for gardening enthusiasts!

Atlanta Apparel Mart   220-3000
250 Spring St. N.W.
Atlanta

Atlanta Sports Carnival. Celebrities from local TV stations join members of the Braves, Hawks and Falcons for an evening of fun. Entertainment includes clowns, magicians, cheerleaders and costumed characters. Special booths are for picture taking with the stars, who also lend their faces to pie throwing, water dunking and games. Fun for the whole family. Children get to meet their sports heroes.

Omni   681-2100
100 Techwood Drive N.W.
Atlanta

Children's Festival. The annual gift to the children of Atlanta from the Woodruff Arts Center is designed to introduce children to the arts. The Atlanta Symphony performs as well as the Atlanta Children's Theatre. There are also puppet shows, clowns, magicians, musical groups, storytelling and strolling characters along with hands-on activities and workshops.

Woodruff Arts Center   892-3600
1280 Peachtree St. N.E.
Atlanta

Goodwill Book Sale. The annual book sale includes hundreds of titles at very affordable prices. Check out the children's book section.

Northlake Mall   938-3564
4800 Briarcliff Road N.E.
Atlanta

Groundhog Day Jugglers' Festival. Children and adults alike will enjoy this early celebration of spring that includes juggling, other forms of object manipulation, magic, balancing and unicycle riding.

Inman Middle School   373-7175
774 Virginia Ave. N.E.
Atlanta

Taste of Chocolate. A must for any chocoholic. Exhibitors offer samples of their products. Products are also available for purchase. Benefits the National Kidney Foundation.

Locations vary   248-1315
Atlanta

March

Atlanta Boat Show. With the largest collection and display of boats in the Southeast, the Atlanta Boat Show is terrific for sailors or would-be boatsmen of all ages. There are fashion shows and fishing and skiing clinics daily.

Georgia World Congress Center   656-7600
285 International Blvd. N.W.
Atlanta

Atlanta Passion Play. Drama and music recreate the week of passion, death, burial and resurrection of Jesus Christ. Not recommended for preschool children.

Atlanta Civic Center   347-8400
395 Piedmont Ave. N.E.
Atlanta

Children's Fishing Derby. Children ages 15 and under fish for trout with prizes awarded for the biggest fish caught. Children must bring their own fishing gear. Ages 10 and under must be accompanied by an adult. Sponsored by the Upper Chattahoochee Chapter of Trout Unlimited.

Chattahoochee River Park   266-0577
Azalea Drive
Roswell

Kaleidoscope. Annual festival for the visual and performing arts sponsored by Cobb County and Marietta Schools. More than 75 performing groups entertain visitors with performances scheduled every 20 minutes.

Cobb County Civic Center   429-3045
548 Clay St. S.E.
Marietta

Kite Flying Contest. Stone Mountain Park's annual competition begins at noon as 2–4 member teams (ages 18 and up) compete to see who can keep their kites up the longest. The 1988 record was 26 hours. Spectators may watch from the top or bottom of the mountain. There is also a designated area for the public to fly kites.

Stone Mountain Park   498-5600
Stone Mountain

St. Patrick's Day Parades. Celebrate the "wearing of the green" with bands, clowns and more. The Hibernian Benevolent Society's annual parade through downtown Atlanta begins at noon. 378-1255.

The Buckhead parade begins and ends at Frankie Allen Park, beginning at 2 p.m. Sponsored by the Friendly Sons of St. Patrick. 952-8745

Youth Symphony Winter Concert. The Atlanta Symphony Youth Orchestra, directed by Jere Flint, performs a program of classical selections. Free.

Symphony Hall   898-1177
1280 Peachtree St. N.E.
Atlanta

Easter

Many Easter egg hunts are traditional within the Atlanta area. Here is a listing of some hunts that have taken place for years.

Atlanta Speech School. Rain or shine. Ages 8 and under. Annual egg hunt with baskets, entertainment and refreshments.

3160 Northside Parkway N.W.   233-5332
Atlanta

Laurel Park. The Easter Bunny visits. Ages 2–8 hunt for candy, prizes and Easter eggs. Sponsored by Marietta Parks and Recreation. No registration required.

151 Manning Road   429-4212
Marietta

Reynolds Nature Preserve. Extra fun time for ages 3–8.

5665 Reynolds Road   961-9257
Morrow

Roswell Department of Recreation. Costume contest first and then children are grouped by age for the hunt. Register by phone or the day of the hunt. Hunt is on the grounds of Herman Miller Inc.

1000 Mansell Road   641-3760

Shorty Howell Park. Children ages 3–7 hunt for eggs. Preregistration required.

2750 Pleasant Hill Road   476-0504
Duluth

Wieuca Road Baptist Church. Ages 12 and under. Register the day of the hunt.

3626 Peachtree Road N.E.   261-4220
Atlanta

April

Atlanta Home Show. More than 500 exhibitors display a wide variety of products for home and garden.

Georgia World Congress Center   656-7600
285 International Blvd. N.W.
Atlanta

Atlanta Hunt and Steeplechase. The Atlanta Steeplechase, part of the Southeastern circuit, brings together horses and riders. Spectators picnic on grassy knolls and dress includes everything from British tweeds to formal morning coats and long dresses.

Cumming   237-7436

Big Shanty Festival. Features a living history village, Civil War re-enactment, arts and crafts, games, rides, children's activities, live entertainment, a parade and the film *The Great Locomotive Chase.*

City of Kennesaw   427-2117
2829 Cherokee St. N.W.
Kennesaw

Brown Bag Concerts. An assortment of upbeat music, dance and other entertainment presented during the noon hour. Free.

Woodruff Park Amphitheater   653-7120
55 Park Place
Atlanta

Celtic Festival. Featuring a showcase of Scottish, Irish and Welsh music, dance, art, theater, folklore and culture. Children's programs include storytelling and other performances.

Oglethorpe University Campus   261-1441
4484 Peachtree Road
Atlanta

Children's Carnival. Especially for preschoolers. Includes games, prizes, food and kid-sized train rides.

Cliff Valley School   321-4367
1911 Cliff Valley Way
Atlanta

Concerts on the Square. A night of family musical entertainment. Free.

Glover Park   429-4212
Marietta

Dogwood Festival. This weekend at Piedmont Park offers something for every member of the family. There are performing and participating events, along with fitness and children's activities. Activities begin on Saturday with a "Razzle-Dazzle Children's Parade." Other activities throughout the weekend include face painting, mural making, rock hunting, hula hoops and costumed characters. The Children's Stage features puppets, magic, music, dance and storytelling. Saturday night is the annual Festival Hot Air Balloon Race.

Piedmont Park   525-6145
Piedmont at 14th St. N.E.
Atlanta

Georgia Renaissance Festival. Features hundreds of costumed characters, live entertainment, authentic hand-made crafts, knights on horseback, musicians, singers, dancers, jugglers, storytellers and plenty of 16th century food.

Exit 12 off I-85 South   964-8575
Fairburn/Peachtree City

Inman Park Festival and Tour. The festival includes a children's fair, bazaar, art show, music and other fun activities. Tour of turn-of-the-century houses.

Inman Park   681-2798
Euclid & Edgewood Avenues N.E.
Atlanta

Kids Carnival. Preschool children and their families enjoy games, pony rides, moonwalk, special entertainers and many more activities.

Shallowford Presbyterian Preschool   321-3061
2375 Shallowford Road
Atlanta

Antebellum Jubilee. Experience the history and culture of the Old South at Stone Mountain Park. The focus of the activities for this celebration is at the Antebellum Plantation, a complex of restored homes and buildings, authentically furnished. Activities include Civil War encampments, 1800's era musical entertainment, traditional Southern storytelling, period arts and crafts demonstrations and open hearth cooking.

Stone Mountain Park   498-5600
Stone Mountain

Sweet Auburn Good Times Festival. Located in the heart of the Auburn Avenue historic district, this downtown event features jazz bands, a parade, a carnival with rides, VIP sports figures and live entertainment.

Auburn Avenue   523-2020
Atlanta

Taste of Atlanta. Annual showcase for Atlanta's most popular restaurants. Loads of food to sample, family fun and even a street dance and party. Gourmet specialties available for purchase. Proceeds benefit the National Kidney Foundation of Georgia.

Southern Bell Center   248-1315
675 West Peachtree St. N.E.
Atlanta

Yaarab Shrine Circus and Carnival. Under the big top, clowns, animals and circus thrills provide entertainment that is sure to delight all ages.

Cobb Central Park   875-0318
2245 Callaway Road
Marietta

May

B.C. Fest. See the world through ancient eyes. At this children's festival, children find out what it was like to live in ancient Greece, Rome, Egypt and Aztec and Mayan cultures.

Emory Museum of Art and Archaeology   727-4282
Emory University Quadrangle
Atlanta

Blue Sky Concert Series. Families enjoy a variety of musical programs on the south lawn of the old courthouse. Bring a blanket, picnic and a friend. Free.

Old Courthouse   371-8386
Downtown Decatur

Brown Bag Concerts. Families bring their lunch and enjoy live entertainment. Free.

Glover Park   429-4212
Marietta

Children's Arts Festival. Hands-on art experience for children with many different workshops available. Sponsored by the Fine Arts Center of Marietta.

Marietta Square   424-8142
Marietta

Concerts on the Square. Bring a blanket, a picnic and a friend. Saturday evenings, 7:30 p.m. Free.

Downtown Decatur   371-8386

Concerts on the Square. A concert series featuring performances ranging from jazz to pops. Free.

Marietta Square   429-4201

DeKalb Sheriff's Posse Rodeo. This World Championship Rodeo features bareback bronco riding, calf roping, barrel racing, steer wrestling, saddle bronc riding and Brahman bull riding.

Stone Mountain Park   498-5600
Stone Mountain

Decatur Artfest. Weekend of art and entertainment. Features Cajun cook-off, an artist market, live performances, children's art festival and food.

Downtown Decatur   371-8386

E. Rivers School Carnival. Games, prizes, pony rides, clowns, spook house, bumper cars and more.

8 Peachtree Battle Ave. N.W.   350-2150
Atlanta

East Atlanta Festival. Day-long festival stage with continuous entertainment. Marionettes, mimes, puppets, music and special children's activity area.

Brownwood Park   627-5462
607 Brownwood Ave. S.E.
Atlanta

Fun Affair. Especially for young children and families. Entertainment ranges from magic tricks and juggling to midway games.

Saint Anne's Episcopal Church   237-7024
3098 Northside Parkway N.W.
Atlanta

Georgia Gem and Mineral Show. Display and sale of rocks, minerals and rare gems found in Georgia and worldwide.

Cobb County Civic Center   429-3045
548 Clay St.
Marietta

Georgia Renaissance Festival. Features hundreds of costumed characters, live entertainment, authentic hand-made crafts, knights on horseback, musicians, singers, dancers, jugglers, storytellers and plenty of 16th century food.

Exit 12 off I-85 South   964-8575
Fairburn/Peachtree City

Kingfest International. Live performances, arts and crafts and food are featured, representing different cultures from around the world.

King Center   524-1956
449 Auburn Ave. N.E.
Atlanta

Laser Show. Begins at Stone Mountain this month. Multicolored laser beams bounce off the mountain and animate popular songs.

Stone Mountain Park   498-5600
Stone Mountain

Snellville Days. Festival features arts and crafts, food and live entertainment.

T. W. Briscoe Park   973-6999
Snellville

Spring Cotton Days. Arts and crafts exhibitors and food concessions are featured.

Glover Park   973-9329
Marietta

Springfest. Clogging, country music, arts and crafts. More than 50 teams participate in an annual barbecue cook-off.

Stone Mountain Park   498-5600
Stone Mountain

Special Olympics. Disabled athletes from throughout Georgia participate in track and field events, aquatics, cycling, gymnastics, soccer, tennis, volleyball and weight lifting. Sponsored by Georgia Special Olympics.

458-3838

Symphony Picnic Concerts. The DeKalb Symphony Orchestra presents outdoor concerts of light classics and popular music on Friday and Saturday evenings.

DeKalb College   299-4136
555 N. Indian Creek Dr.
Clarkston

Wren's Nest Fest. Features storytellers, jugglers, clowns, musicians, Royal Punch and Judy puppets and Atlanta Street Theatre.

1050 Gordon St. S.W.   753-8535
Atlanta

Youth Orchestra Spring Concert. The Atlanta Symphony Youth Orchestra performs various musical pieces.

Woodruff Arts Center   892-2414
1280 Peachtree St. N.E.
Atlanta

West End Festival. Arts, crafts, food vendors and a wide variety of music—jazz, gospel, reggae, Latin and Caribbean.

West End Park   752-9329
West End Ave.
Atlanta

June

Annual Neighbor Day. Families can see an airport up close. There are antique airplanes, corporate jets, helicopters and ultralight aircraft. Displays, exhibits and booths provide information about everything from whirlybirds to emergency medical care, along with aerial demonstrations with aircraft fly-bys and aerobatic performances.

DeKalb-Peachtree Airport   457-7236
Clairmont Road
Chamblee

Ashley Whippet International. Teams of Frisbee throwers and their disk-catching dogs compete for points and a chance to go to the finals.

Laurel Park   429-4220
151 Manning Road
Marietta

Atlanta Jazz Series. Live jazz performances. Free.

Piedmont Park 653-7146	Grant Park 653-7146
Piedmont at 14th St. N.E.	537 Park Ave. S.E.
Atlanta	Atlanta

Atlanta Symphony Concerts. Concerts feature an evening of light classical music under the stars. Free.

Piedmont Park 892-2414	Grant Park 892-2414
Piedmont at 14th St. N.E.	537 Park Ave. S.E.
Atlanta	Atlanta

Celebrate Israel. Festival features an Israeli marketplace, hands-on arts and crafts, theater production, petting zoo, pony rides, singing and dancing, Maccabean games and authentic foods of Israel.

Zaban Park   875-7881
5342 Tilly Mill Road
Dunwoody

Decatur Beach Party. Downtown Decatur is turned into a beach complete with sand, waves, lifeguards and palm trees. Also features special beach area for children, beach music, limbo contests and plenty of food.

Downtown Decatur   371-8386

Fox Theatre Summer Film Festival. Family films are shown in the manner of an old-fashioned Saturday matinee, with sing-alongs and vintage cartoons.

660 Peachtree St. N.E.   881-2100
Atlanta

Kidsfest. Clowns, magicians, games, face painters and cartoon characters are on hand to provide extra entertainment.

White Water   424-9283
250 N. Cobb Parkway N.E.
Marietta

Kingfest. Annual arts festival at the King Center takes place every other weekend on Saturdays and Sundays. Song, dance, poetry, storytelling, theater, comedy and juggling. Kids Day held in June.

449 Auburn Ave. N.E.   524-1956
Atlanta

Living History Program. A Civil War encampment with living history demonstrations.

Kennesaw Mountain National Battlefield Park   427-4686
Old Highway 41
Marietta

Living History Weekend. Experience what a day in 1862 would have been like. Included are a Confederate camp, Southern belles, demonstrations of how butter was churned and candles were made and a battle scene.

Lanier Museum of Natural History   945-3543
2601 Buford Dam Road
Buford

Peachtree Junior Road Race. This 3K (2-mile) race is for children ages 7–12 and allows the children to enjoy the excitement and prestige of the Peachtree. Sponsored by the Atlanta Track Club.

Piedmont Park   231-9064
Atlanta

Possum Trot. One-mile fun run and 10K race.

Chattahoochee Nature Center   992-2055
9135 Willeo Road
Roswell

Spring Dance Concert. Young dancers of the Apprentice Dance Company present work by professional choreographers as well as original choreography by the members themselves.

Callanwolde Fine Arts Center   872-5338
980 Briarcliff Road N.E.
Atlanta

Summer Candlelight Concerts. The performers of Cobb High School's "Electricity" present a program of jazz, rock and country music. Enjoy an evening of music with a picnic. Free.

Mable House   739-0189
5239 Floyd Road
Mableton

Summer Concerts on the Square. Concert series featuring performances ranging from jazz to pops. Free.

Marietta Square   429-4201

Summerfest at Grant Park. Live and recorded music along with carnival games, balloons and Frisbees highlight this family–oriented festival.

537 Park Ave. S.E.   627-9751
Atlanta

July

Atlanta Jazz Series. Bring a picnic and enjoy jazz at its best. Free.

Piedmont Park   653-7146
Piedmont at 14th St. N.E.
Atlanta

Grant Park   653-7146
537 Park Ave. S.E.
Atlanta

Atlanta Symphony Concert. Features an evening of light classical music. Free.

Piedmont Park   892-241 4
Piedmont at 14th St. N.E.
Atlanta

Callanwolde Concert Band. Bring blankets and a picnic and enjoy a summer evening of music under the stars. Free.

980 Briarcliff Road N.E.   872-5338
Atlanta

Candlelite Concerts. Programs featuring many musical styles. Free.

Mable House   739-0189
5239 Floyd Road
Mableton

Fox Theatre Summer Film Festival. Family films shown in the manner of an old-fashioned Saturday matinee, with sing-alongs and vintage cartoons.

660 Peachtree St. N.E.   881-2100
Atlanta

Georgia Shakespeare Festival. See May listing.

Kingfest. Every other weekend until August, this festival features a wide variety of musical performers, arts and crafts, dance, theater, poetry, mime and puppetry performances. Free.

449 Auburn Ave. N.E.   524-1956
Atlanta

Living History Weekend. Living history program including a Civil War re-enactment along with other demonstrations and war era music.

Kennesaw Mountain National Battlefield Park   427-4686
Old Highway 41
Marietta

Puppetry Arts Festival. Six-week summer festival features a different production each week.

Center for Puppetry Arts   873-3391
1404 Spring St. N.W.
Atlanta

Stay and See Georgia. Annual event that features more than 50 exhibitors from all over Georgia to promote Georgia's cities, festivals, parks, historical sites and more. Live entertainment. Free.

Underground Atlanta   651-9464

Summer Concert. Cobb Symphony Orchestra presents an evening of classical music. Free.

Galleria Amphitheater   988-9641 or 859-1200
Behind Galleria Specialty Mall
Atlanta

Summer Friday Night Concert Series. Bring a picnic and enjoy the sounds.

Glover Park   429-4212
Marietta

July 4 Celebrations

Alpharetta. Arts and crafts show, games, entertainment and old-fashioned barbecue at Wills Park.

350 Marietta Street   751-7262
Alpharetta

Atlanta Downtown Parade. Salute 2 America Parade is the largest Independence Day Parade in the country with more than 100 bands and floats. Starts at the Omni Hotel on Marietta Street, then turns down Peachtree Street to Ralph McGill Boulevard.

897-7385

Atlanta-Lenox Square. Live entertainment, mimes, clowns and jugglers along with the Army Ground Forces Band from Ft. McPherson.

3393 Peachtree Road N.E.   233-6767
Atlanta

Callaway Gardens. Enjoy family activities all day, including live entertainment, and end the evening with fireworks and a laser show.

Pine Mountain, Georgia   1-800-282-8181

Cobb County Civic Center. Pop Concert.

548 Clay Street   429-3045
Marietta

Galleria. Free concert.

Atlanta   988-9641

Decatur. Pied Piper Parade is filled with children being pushed and pulled to the courthouse in their favorite wheeled toy. Concert on the Courthouse Square and fireworks complete the day.

371-8386

Kennesaw. Road race, baseball tournament and watermelon eating. Fireworks at dusk.

Adams Park   424-8274
Park Drive
Kennesaw

Lake Lanier Islands. Live concert followed by fireworks at Wildwaves.

6950 Holiday Road   945-6701
Lake Lanier Islands, GA

Marietta. Parade down Roswell Street, as well as food fairs, carnival games, music and live entertainment. Free.

429-4212

Peachtree Road Race. Annual 10K race that begins at Lenox Square and goes down Peachtree Road to Piedmont Park.

231-9064
Atlanta

Stone Mountain Park. Fantastic Fourth. Concerts, fireworks, beach activities, as well as mimes, jugglers, clowns and cloggers entertain the whole family.

Stone Mountain   498-5600

Tucker. Happy Birthday America Parade with children riding tricycles, scooters, bikes, etc. Patriotic music and refreshments add to the fun. Free.

938-5022

Fireworks

Alpharetta-Wills Park
Atlanta-Atlanta-Fulton County Stadium,
      Lenox Square
Callaway Gardens
Decatur-Courthouse Square
Kennesaw-Adams Park

Lake Lanier Islands
Lilburn-Marketplace Shopping Center
Peachtree City-Picnic Park
Six Flags
Smyrna-Kings Park, Talleson Park
Stone Mountain Park

August

Atlanta Symphony Orchestra Concert. Bring a blanket and picnic and enjoy light classical favorites performed by the Atlanta Symphony Orchestra. Free.

Piedmont Park   892-2414
Piedmont at 14th St. N.E.
Atlanta

National Black Arts Festival. This biennial event takes place throughout the city and includes puppet shows, theater and dance presentations, films and workshops.

730-7315

Callanwolde Concert Band. Bring a blanket and picnic and enjoy music under the stars.

Callanwolde Arts Center   872-5338
980 Briarcliff Road N.E.
Atlanta

Children's Art Festival. A variety of performances and hands-on children's activities.

Kennesaw Depot   424-6152
Across from Big Shanty Museum
Cherokee Street
Kennesaw

Diaper Derby. Not a beauty contest, but a chance to show off your baby. Age division from newborn to 6 months and 7-12 months. Awards for the most hair, least hair, unique dress, biggest eyes, etc. Includes a rattle race for toddlers. Sponsored by Marietta Parks and Recreation.

Cobb County Civic Center   429-4212
548 Clay St. S.E.
Marietta

Festival of the Painted Rock. Chattahoochee Nature Center's annual festival includes fine arts and crafts, musical entertainment, food and children's activities such as clowns, face painting and art corner.

9135 Willeo Road   992-2055
Roswell

Friday Night Concert. Live music on the square. Free.

Glover Park   429-4212
Marietta

Georgia Shakespeare Festival. See May listing.

Kingfest. Annual arts festival at the King Center continues every other weekend and features music, dance, theater, poetry, puppetry and mime as well as arts and crafts. Free.

449 Auburn Ave. N.E.   524-1956
Atlanta

Living History Weekend. A Confederate camp is set up and Southern belles are in full costume. Skirmishes between the North and the South are staged throughout the day.

Lanier Museum of Natural History   945-3543
2601 Bufurd Dam Road
Buford

Summer Concert Series. A variety of music.

Galleria Amphitheater   988-9641 or 859-1200
Behind Galleria Specialty Mall
Atlanta

September

Art in the Park. Original artwork plus live entertainment. Free.
Glover Park   429-4212
Marietta

Arts Festival of Atlanta. Annual event includes visual and performing arts, a festive market of more than 250 juried artists, a youth art exhibit and special children's activities.

Piedmont Park   885-1125
Piedmont at 14th St. N.E.
Atlanta

Baby Expo. A weekend of family fun, including fashion shows, prizes, baby crawl-off, toddler Olympics and more.

Georgia World Congress Center   266-0997
285 International Blvd. N.W.
Atlanta

Big Wheel Rally. Children, ages 3-7, enjoy racing, spinning out and driving the obstacle course in their Big Wheels. Free.

Laurel Park   429-4212
151 Manning Road
Marietta

Brown Bag Concerts. Live entertainment from noon until 1 p.m. Bring a lunch and enjoy the sounds.

Glover Park   429-4212
Marietta

Concerts on the Square. Series of concerts featuring a variety of music. Free.

Downtown Decatur on the Square   371-8386

Elizabeth Reinhardt

Garden Hills Ice Cream Social. Ice cream, hot dogs, arts and crafts, games, rides, contests for children and fun for the entire family.

Sunnybrook Park   240-0305
Between East Wesley and Rumson Roads
Atlanta

Georgia Music Festival. A variety of musical entertainment. Free.

Various sites   656-3551

Greek Festival. Music, dancing, exhibits, plus all kinds of Greek dinners and pastries are available.

Greek Orthodox Cathedral   633-7358
2500 Clairmont Road N.E.
Atlanta

Gwinnett County Fair. An old-fashioned fair with animal exhibits (cattle, sheep, rabbits, pigs, etc.), a flower show, a beauty pageant and entertainment that includes clogging and music.

Gwinnett Fairgrounds   963-6522
Off Highway 20
Lawrenceville

Labor Day Bluegrass Jamboree. A celebration of musical heritage with bluegrass concerts featuring bands from all over the South.

Fort Yargo State Park   1-404-867-3489
Winder

Montreux Atlanta International Music Festival. A variety of music genres presented throughout the city. Main shows are at Piedmont Park.

Piedmont at 14th St. N.E.   653-7160
Atlanta

North Georgia State Fair. Family fun stage shows, music, food, exhibits, Kiddie Land, petting zoo, exotic bird show, Rapid Razorback Racing Pigs and midway rides.

Central Park   428-1300
2245 Callaway Road
Marietta

Riverfest. Festival features more than 100 artists and craftspeople, demonstrations, children's activity area, entertainment and food.

Boling Park   1-404-479-81331
Canton

Roswell Arts Festival. This event features continuous performing arts along with displays of arts and crafts for sale.

Towne Square   641-3765
Roswell

Sesame Street Live. Big Bird and his Sesame Street friends entertain young children.

Omni   681-2100
100 Techwood Drive N.W.
Atlanta

Ye Olde English Festival. Recapture the charm and magic of Renaissance England with local groups performing music, dance and drama. A special area for children with pony rides, space walk, puppet show, face painting, games, storytelling, musicians and more.

St. Bartholomew's Church   634-3336
1790 Lavista Road N.E.
Atlanta

Yellow Daisy Arts and Crafts Festival. More than 400 fine arts and crafts, two stages of continuous entertainment, festival food, a flower show and more.

Stone Mountain Park   498-5600
Stone Mountain

October

All-American Mutt Show. Celebrate Adopt-a-Dog Month by entering your mutt in this unique dog show. Categories include largest, smallest, most like owner and All-American Mutt. Sponsored by the Atlanta Humane Society. Free to spectators.

Chastain Park   875-5331
135 W. Wieuca Road N.W.
Atlanta

Art Fest. Theater performances, a balloon release, artists' market, children's carnival and more.

Steeple House Arts Center   952-8661
300 Village Place
Marietta

Arts and Crafts on Peachtree. Annual festival includes arts and crafts, entertainment, magicians, clowns, singers and dancers. Sponsored by the Pilot Club with proceeds benefiting area charities.

E. Rivers School   350-2150
8 Peachtree Battle Ave. N.W.
Atlanta

Arts in the Park. Fall festival featuring handmade arts and crafts, antiques, collectibles and food.

T.W. Briscoe Park   972-0200
2500 Sawyer Parkway
Snellville

Atlanta International School Fall Festival. Games, toy store, space walk, clowns, face painting, a haunted room and varied activities. Also, an international bazaar with arts and crafts and international foods.

4820 Long Island Drive N.W.   843-3380
Atlanta

Atlanta Symphony Family Concert. A program of light classical music for the family.

Symphony Hall   892-2414
1280 Peachtree St. N.E.
Atlanta

Autumn Arts and Crafts Festival. Face painting, music, children's activities and other entertainment are included in the festivities.

Tucker Recreation Center   938-5383
4898 Lavista Road
Tucker

Celebrating the Creative Arts. Visual and performing arts, scarecrow making, face painting, T-shirt painting, mimes, clowns, magicians and more.

Druid Hills Presbyterian Church   875-7591
1026 Ponce de Leon Ave. N.E.
Atlanta

Fernbank Fall Festival. Features a bird walk, 5K race, marketplace of science-oriented gifts, children's planetarium show, chemistry demonstrations, laboratory open houses and talks on many natural topics.

156 Heaton Park Drive N.E.   378-4311
Atlanta

Festival by the River. Festival features fine arts and crafts, live entertainment, storytellers, music, dance, magicians, art activities for children and more.

Pinckneyville Arts Center   449-5910
4300 Holcomb Bridge Road
Norcross

Folklife Festival. The Atlanta History Center presents this annual festival at the Tullie Smith farmhouse complex. Costumed craftspeople transport visitors back in time to an 1840s Piedmont Georgia farm with demonstrations. Visitors can try their hand at butter churning, spinning, weaving, quilting and making music on traditional instruments.

3101 Andrews Drive N.W.   261-1837
Atlanta

Heiskell School Fall Festival. Games, pony rides, prizes and more.

3260 Northside Drive N.W.   262-2233
Atlanta

Heritage Days. Craft demonstrations, old-fashioned games, 1800s fashion show, arts and crafts booths and a Civil War re-enactment.

Lanier Museum of Natural History   945-3543
2601 Buford Dam Road
Buford

Human Sexuality Week. Fernbank Science Center presents its annual series of programs for parents and their children. Topics include puberty and adolescence (age 11), embryology for families (ages 5–8) and sexually transmitted diseases (ages 12 and older).

156 Heaton Park Drive N.E.   378-4311
Atlanta

Immaculate Heart of Mary Fall Festival. Children's games, entertainment, a spook house, food and more.

2855 Briarcliff Road N.E.   636-4488
Atlanta

Lilburn Daze. Arts and crafts, food, clowns and much more.

Lilburn City Park   921-2210
Lilburn

Minor Elementary Fall Festival. Arts and crafts, carnival games, prizes, Minor Taste of Gwinnett and auction highlight this festival.

4129 Shady Drive   925-9543
Lilburn

Octoberfest. Live entertainment, games, rides, hot-air balloons, pony rides and more. Sponsored by Telephone Pioneers of America to benefit area charities.

6701 Roswell Road   391-2693
Atlanta

Scottish Highland Games. Annual gathering of the clans includes sporting competitions, band contests, Scottish heritage and bagpipes, pipes and drum music.

Stone Mountain Park   396-5728
Stone Mountain

Youth Day Festival. A week of activities honoring Roswell youth. A parade of youth groups, floats, bands and more.

Woodstock Road   641-3760
Roswell

Halloween

Atlanta Humane Society. Children of all ages enjoy storytellers, magicians, puppets and costumed characters. Activities include a costume contest with prizes.

981 Howell Mill Road N.W.   873-5564
Atlanta

Briarwood Center. Separate carnivals for ages 3–5 and ages 6–12. Lots of carnival games for fun and prizes. Certificate and ribbons for winners.

2235 Briarwood Way N.E.   636-1933
Atlanta

Decatur Recreation Center. Halloween fun for preschoolers to school-age children includes storytelling, carnival games, prizes, clowns and a space walk. Decatur residents only.

231 Sycamore St.   377-0494
Decatur

"Fright Night" at Six Flags. All areas of the park are transformed into a spine-tingling arena full of hair-raising family fun and entertainment.

7561 Six Flags Road S.E.   789-3400
Austell

Glover Park. Halloween activities and live entertainment.

Marietta   429-4212

Great Halloween Caper at Zoo Atlanta. Trick or treat with the animals. Also costume contest, candy and Halloween photos for children.
Grant Park   624-5678
800 Cherokee Ave. S.E.
Atlanta

Gresham Park Center. A carnival with fun and games and prizes. Open to children under age 12. Costumes are encouraged.
3113 Gresham Road S.E.   241-2616
Atlanta

Hamilton Center. Ages 12 and under enjoy fun and games and a haunted house along with candy and prizes.
Chapel Street   299-1046
Scottsdale

Laurel Park. Children play carnival games, scurry through the Haunted Forest and the Land of Make-Believe.
151 Manning Road   429-4211
Marietta

Pace Academy Fair. Family-oriented activities for all ages. Children's games, haunted house, goodies walk, pony rides and teen center.
966 W. Paces Ferry Road N.W.   262-1345
Atlanta

Peachtree Road United Methodist Church. Carnival includes a haunted house, cake walk, more than 20 booths, games and plenty of treats for all ages.
3180 Peachtree Road N.E.   266-2386
Atlanta

Roswell Road Community Activity Building. Halloween party for the physically handicapped includes carnival games and costume contest. Also separate carnival for preschool–age 6 and ages 7-11. Features haunted house and costume contest.
Woodstock Road   641-3760
Roswell

Tour of Southern Ghosts. Storytelling festival for Halloween. Tour the grounds of the Antebellum Plantation and meet different storytellers who intrigue visitors with famous and infamous ghost stories. Refreshments and fortune tellers round out the evening.
Stone Mountain Park   498-5600
Stone Mountain

Tucker Recreation Center. Separate parties for children ages 3-6 and ages 7 and up. Both parties include games, face painting, fortune telling and more.
4898 Lavista Road   938-5383
Tucker

Lithonia. Separate carnivals for ages 3-5 and ages 6-13. Costume contests, prizes and games.
2484 Bruce St.   482-0405
Lithonia

Lullwater School. Games, a haunted house (designed and operated by children for children), food and fun for elementary-age children.
705 S. Candler St.   378-6643
Decatur

Haunted Houses

Cumberland Mall. An evening of spine-chilling entertainment. This 40-minute tour takes visitors through 30 rooms rigged with optical illusions and special effects.

1000 Cumberland Mall N.W.   435-2206
Atlanta

Rhodes Hall. This Atlanta landmark is transformed into a haunted house extraordinaire. Not recommended for easily frightened children.

1516 Peachtree St. N.W.   881-9980
Atlanta

November

Arts and Crafts Festival. St. John Newman Church presents its annual festival that features food, 50 arts and crafts booths, a children's area and more.

801 Tom Smith Road   923-6633
Lilburn

Atlanta Symphony Family Concert. A show of light classical music for the whole family.

Symphony Hall   892-2414
1280 Peachtree St. N.E.
Atlanta

Atlanta Symphony Youth Orchestra Concert. Jere Flint conducts the Youth Orchestra, which is composed of musicians ages 14–17, in its annual fall concert.

Symphony Hall   892-2414
1280 Peachtree St. N.E.
Atlanta

Chestnut Ridge Christian Church Fall Festival. Crafts, a bake sale, quilt raffle, children's activity area and more.

2663 Johnson Ferry Road   971-8888
Marietta

Christmas at Callanwolde. See December listing.

Christmas House. St. Andrews Presbyterian Preschool presents its annual event that includes a craft and gift bazaar, a "secret shop," food and a visit from Santa.

4882 Lavista Road   934-1461
Tucker

Christmas in Gwinnett. Holiday arts and crafts show presented by the Creative Arts and Crafts Guild.

Best Friend Park   449-3750
6224 Jimmy Carter Blvd.
Norcross

Holiday Celebration. See December listing.

Minority School Fair. Minority Atlanta Families in Independent Schools sponsors representatives from area schools, as well as boarding schools to answer questions about schools, admission procedures and financial aid.

Woodward Academy   393-9230 or 471-5238
1662 Rugby Ave.
College Park

Nutcracker Ballet. The dancers of Southeastern Dance Theatre present this holiday ballet classic.

256-1056

Nutcracker Ballet. This holiday classic will be presented by the professional and apprentice dancers of Ruth Mitchell Dance Theatre.

426-0007

Rich's Department Store Tree Lighting. Every Thanksgiving evening, Rich's lights its giant Christmas tree, signaling the beginning of the Christmas season in Atlanta. Choirs sing carols and other pre-yuletide festivities. The lighting of the tree can be viewed from both ends of Forsyth Street.

Forsyth Street near Marietta Street   586-2551
Atlanta

Santa Arrives. At most area shopping malls.

Studio 13 Fall Festival. Arts and craft show with more than 94 exhibitors.

Cobb County Civic Center   429-3045
548 Clay Street
Marietta

Veterans Day Parade. More than 200 units including marching bands, clowns, floats, military vehicles and elected officials honor our country's veterans. Parade begins at Peachtree at West Peachtree and proceeds south on Peachtree toward Woodruff Park.

Atlanta   321-6111

December

Atlanta Boys Choir Concerts. Several concerts are scheduled for the holiday season.
378-0064

Atlanta Christmas Pageant. More than 200 adults and children perform in a costumed production accompanied by a 25-piece orchestra and bell choir.
Second Ponce de Leon Baptist Church   266-8111
2715 Peachtree Road N.E.
Atlanta

Atlanta Symphony Concert. A delightful program filled with carols and other holiday music.
Symphony Hall   892-2414
1280 Peachtree St. N.E.
Atlanta

Boy Scout Show. This show takes up three exhibit halls, along with an outdoor exhibit.
Georgia World Congress Center   656-7600
285 International Blvd. N.W.
Atlanta

Breakfast with Santa. A nutritious breakfast, along with a visit from Santa and other surprises.
Macy's Peachtree   221-7882
180 Peachtree St. N.W.
Atlanta

Candlelight Tour of Homes. See beautifully restored turn-of-the-century homes decorated for the holidays in historic Grant Park.
Grant Park Learning Center   521-0418
Atlanta

Christmas at Callanwolde. Atlanta's interior designers decorate the rooms and halls of the mansion in seasonal splendor. Includes shops, a gallery, cafe and live entertainment.
Callanwolde Arts Center   872-5338
980 Briarcliff Road N.E.
Atlanta

Christmas Home Tour. Tour of several restored 19th century homes filled with decorations of Christmases past.
Kennesaw Avenue Historic District   429-1115
Kennesaw

Christmas Then and Now. Catch the spirit of Christmas past and present at the Bowman-Pirkle Homestead, decorated in the style of the mid-1800s.
Lanier Museum of Natural History   945-3543
2601 Buford Dam Road
Buford

Cobb Symphony Orchestra Concert. Holiday concert.
Cobb County Civic Center   429-3045
548 Clay St.
Marietta

Macy's-Egleston Christmas Parade

Country Christmas. The grounds are adorned with holiday decorations, wreaths, greenery and a giant tree. Also carolers, live entertainment, carriage rides, chestnut roasting, arts and crafts and Santa.

Atlanta Botanical Gardens   876-5858
Piedmont Road at the Prado
Atlanta

Family Festival. Sponsored by the Goethe Institute. Festival filled with family fun and live entertainment including puppets, dancers, choral groups, magicians, storytellers, animals and Santa.

Colony Square   892-2388
400 Colony Square N.E.
Atlanta

Family Tree Lighting. Holiday concert and lighting of Decatur tree.

Downtown Decatur   371-8386

Fantasy of Lights. The zoo is set aglow with thousands of lights, live entertainment, craft demonstrations, holiday food, Santa and more. Also visiting reindeer, camel rides and Santa's Workshop.

Zoo Atlanta   624-5678
800 Cherokee St.
Atlanta

Festival of Trees. Includes designer trees, wreaths, vignettes, gingerbread houses, children's activities, international holiday displays, secret gift shop, other holiday shopping, Santa and live entertainment. Benefits Henrietta Egleston Hospital for Children.

Georgia World Congress Center   264-9348
285 International Blvd. N.W.
Atlanta

Holiday Celebration. Parkwide decorations and a large Tree of Lights on the top of the mountain. Also, carriage rides, candlelight tours of the antebellum plantation, Santa's workshop, live entertainment, storytellers, choral groups and special laser show.

Stone Mountain Park   498-5600

Holiday in the Park. The park is transformed into a winter wonderland with elaborate decorations, live musical show, carolers, strolling bands, ski jumping, ice skating, festive food and gifts.

Six Flags Over Georgia   739-3440
7561 Six Flags Road S.E.
Austell

Living Nativity Scene. The story of the first Christmas is dramatized with music and live animals.

Rockspring Presbyterian Church   875-7483
1824 Piedmont Ave. N.E.
Atlanta

Nutcracker Ballet. The Atlanta Ballet presents its annual production of this holiday classic.

Atlanta Civic Center   873-5811
395 Piedmont Ave. N.E.
Atlanta

Puppet Pursuit. Special hands-on exhibit to delight children of all ages.

Center for Puppetry Arts   873-3391
1404 Spring St. N.W.
Atlanta

Macy's-Egleston Christmas Parade. One of the largest parades in the Southeast. Parade begins at Edgewood and Peachtree and ends at West Peachtree and Pine Street. More than 100 clowns, storybook characters, award-winning bands, floats and Santa.

Downtown Atlanta   222-2127

Rich's Pink Pig. A holiday tradition in Atlanta. Priscilla and Percival Pig ride a rooftop track at Rich's downtown store. Children will also get a close-up view of the giant tree with its basketball-sized ornaments.

45 Broad St. S.W.   586-4489
Atlanta

Smoke Rise. More than 200 crafters display and sell their wares.

Smoke Rise Elementary   939-6714
1991 Silver Hill Road
Stone Mountain

Teddy Bear Tea. Children, along with their favorite teddy bears, and parents enjoy tea, hot chocolate and gingerbread cookies.

Ritz-Carlton   659-0400
181 Peachtree St. N.E.
Atlanta

Yule Log Festivities. Includes a candlelight walk through the woods as well as gathering around the traditional yule log fire for singing and storytelling.

Reynolds Nature Preserve   961-9257
5665 Reynolds Road
Morrow

MUSEUMS AND HISTORICAL SITES

SciTrek

E xciting, entertaining, educational and fun—that's Atlanta's museums. If dad is a Civil War buff, junior is an aviation enthusiast, mom is into archaeology and sis likes dolls, not to worry. Whatever your interests, you will be pleasantly surprised at what Atlanta's museums and historical sites have to offer.

African American Panoramic Experience (APEX)

This museum, housed in a beautifully restored 1910 building, features pictorial exhibits of famous black businessmen and residents of "Sweet Auburn" Avenue. Utilizing multimedia displays of sights and sounds, visitors walk through the Afro-American experience from early Africa to present day America. The museum also features a collection of African art and traveling exhibits.

135 Auburn Ave. N.E.   521-2739
Tuesday-Saturday 10 a.m.-5 p.m., Sunday 1-5 p.m.
Open Wednesday until 6 p.m.
Adults, $2; children, $1

Antebellum Plantation House

This beautiful antebellum plantation will give children a real step back in history. The house is decorated with authentic furnishings and antiques, and the outbuildings are carefully identified and described.

Stone Mountain Park   498-5600
10 a.m.-8 p.m. daily
Winter hours: 10 a.m.-5 p.m.
Adults, $2.50; children 3-11, $1.50
Parking permit: one day, $5; annual fee, $20

Antique Auto and Music Museum

Classic car buffs of all ages will delight in this gleaming collection of vintage cars (more than 30). For antique lovers, there's a variety of nickelodeons and an antique carousel.

Stone Mountain Park   498-5600
10 a.m.-9 p.m. daily
Winter hours: 10 a.m.-5 p.m.
Adults, $2.50; children 3-11, $1.50
Parking permit is required

Atlanta Heritage Row

Opened in fall 1990, the 7,000-square-foot building houses six history exhibits and presents "The Spirit of Atlanta" on high-definition television. The walk-through exhibits echo with train whistles, Martin Luther King Jr. speeches and the sounds of an airplane cockpit. Kids will line up to crouch in a Civil War bomb shelter, climb through a 1920s trolley car and enter a Delta cockpit. In addition, information about many of Atlanta's other historical attractions will be available here.

Underground Atlanta   584-7879
Tuesday-Saturday 10 a.m.-7 p.m., Sunday 1-7 p.m.
Adults, $4; students and seniors, $3; children 3-12, $2

Carter Presidential Center

Located on a hilltop overlooking Atlanta, the Carter Presidential Center includes a Japanese garden, waterfalls and a lake. Inside are exhibits on life in the White House, including a replica of the Oval Office and several exhibits on the life and presidency of Carter. A 30-minute film, "President," is shown on the history of the office, and a touch-sensory video screen allows visitors to "ask" the president questions.

One Copenhill Ave. N.E.   420-5100
Atlanta
Monday-Saturday 9 a.m.-4:45 p.m., Sunday noon-4:45 p.m.
Adults, $2.50; seniors, $1.50; children 16 and younger, free

Center for Puppetry Arts Museum

This unique museum gives an overview of the history of puppets and features the largest private collection of puppets in the country. From Punch and Judy to the Muppets, from ritualistic African figures to Chinese hand puppets, from the past to the present, you'll be enchanted!

1404 Spring St. N.W.   873-3391
Atlanta
Monday-Saturday 9 a.m.-4 p.m.
$2

Cobb County Youth Museum

Designed especially for children, this participatory museum features changing historical exhibits. Through the use of skits, costumes and puppet shows, guests are actively involved in the tour. The museum is reserved for Cobb County school children during the week from September through May.

649 Cheatham Drive S.W.   427-2563
Marietta
Call for specific Sundays and summer days when they are open to outside groups
$1 donation

Cyclorama

The Cyclorama is a dramatic 50-foot-high, 400-foot circular painting depicting the Battle of Atlanta. The canvas is enhanced by three-dimensional figures, lighting and sound effects. Visitors sit in theater-style seats on a rotating platform as they listen to narration about the battle. The museum also features a film, the locomotive "Texas," Civil War exhibits and a large, extensive bookstore.

300 Cherokee Ave. S.E.   658-7625
9:30 a.m.-5:30 p.m. daily
Adults, $3.50; seniors, $3; children 6-12, $2; under 6, free

DeKalb County Historical Society Museum

In the old courthouse on the square in Decatur is the DeKalb Historical Society head-quarters. The museum displays clothing, furniture, household articles, farming implements and photos. A short distance from the courthouse, the society has restored an 1822 log cabin and an antebellum town house. There is also a walking tour of 20 sights that will take you past Agnes Scott College, the Decatur Railroad Depot and the Decatur Cemetery.

Old Courthouse on the Square   373-1088
Decatur
Monday-Friday 9 a.m.-4 p.m.
Free admission

Emory University Museum of Art and Archeology

Where can you find an Egyptian mummy for the kids to ogle? The Emory Museum. Housed in a classic marble building, the museum permanently displays mummies and ancient Mediterranean and Middle Eastern artifacts, such as pottery, bronzes, glass vessels, cuneiform tablets, coins and sculpture.

Michael C. Carolos Hall   727-7522
Emory University Quadrangle
Atlanta
Tuesday-Saturday 10 a.m.-4:30 p.m., Sunday noon-5 p.m.
$2 donation

Emory University Mineral and Geology Collection

Self-guided tour of minerals and gems of Georgia and around the world. The collection is labeled and on display.

First floor of the Geology building   727-6491
1557 Pierce Drive
Atlanta
Monday-Friday 8:30 a.m.-5 p.m.
Free admission

Federal Reserve Bank Monetary Museum

Youngsters with coin collections or Scouts who want to earn merit badges should be steered toward the Money Museum. The three-part exhibit traces the evolution of money, shows money in America and includes a numismatic section. Among the artifacts exhibited are trade beads, beaver pelts and a 27-pound gold bar. You can even help yourself to some shredded money!

104 Marietta St. N.W.   521-8764
Atlanta
Monday-Friday 9 a.m.-4 p.m. (groups larger than 10, call for appointment)
Free admission

Fort Peachtree

This is the site of a fort/trading post that was built in the early 1800s as a defense against Creek Indians. The reconstructed log cabin now houses Indian artifacts and historic documents.

2630 Ridgewood Road N.W.   355-7310
Atlanta
Monday-Friday 8 a.m.-4 p.m., reservations required
Free admission

J. C. Gazaway Indian Museum

This museum, located in a log cabin, holds a personal collection of hundreds of Indian artifacts, arrowheads, pottery and more. Many of the Indian relics are from the Cherokee Indians that used to live in Georgia. There are also Indian artifacts from South American tribes.

Lower Creighton Road off Highway 369   1-404-887-2586
Cumming
Saturday and Sunday 9 a.m.-5 p.m.
Donations accepted

Georgia Department of Archives and History

This windowless building that looks like a huge block of marble contains official state records, genealogical resources, maps and many other documents. An exhibit in the lobby illustrates the history of the state, and stained glass windows depict the rise and fall of the Confederacy.

330 Capitol Ave. S.E.   656-2350
Atlanta
Monday–Friday 8 a.m.–4:15 p.m., Saturday 9:30 a.m.–3:15 p.m.
Free admission

Georgia State Capitol

Visitors to the State Museum at the Capitol will find information and enjoyment. Wildlife dioramas on the first floor follow the theme of "A Walk Through Georgia." There is a large collection of Indian artifacts, guns, flags and portraits and busts of famous Georgians.

Capitol Hill and Washington Street   656-2844
Atlanta
Monday–Friday 8 a.m.–5:30 p.m., Saturday 10 a.m.–2 p.m., Sunday 1-3 p.m.
Free admission

The Herndon Home

Alonzo Herndon was a former slave who rose to prominence and wealth as the founder of the Atlanta Life Insurance Co. The Herndon Home, built in 1910, is an elegant 15-room Beaux Arts Classical mansion. On display in the home are antique furnishings, fine silver, Roman and Venetian glass, historical photographs and decorative artwork.

587 University Place N.W.   581-9813
Atlanta
Tuesday–Saturday 10 a.m.–4 p.m.
Free admission

High Museum of Art

High Museum of Art

Richard Meier designed this incredible museum, which houses paintings, sculpture, decorative arts, photography and many exciting traveling exhibitions. The younger set will particularly enjoy "Spectacles," the children's exhibit on the lower floor. Here children are free to experience art as they learn about concepts such as color, light, space and texture. The video installation, art felt wall and studio gallery all encourage active participation.

1280 Peachtree St. N.E.   892-3600
Atlanta
Tuesday-Saturday 10 a.m.-5 p.m., Wednesday 10 a.m.-9 p.m., Sunday noon-5 p.m.
Adults, $4; children 6-17, $1 (no charge on Thursday)

High Museum at Georgia-Pacific

This beautiful "greenhouse" museum received the American Institute of Architects Award. It displays major works from the main museum, as well as traveling exhibits.

133 Peachtree St. N.E.   577-6940
Atlanta
Monday-Friday 11 a.m.-5 p.m.
Free admission

Inman Park and Trolley Barn

Inman Park, Atlanta's oldest suburb, is adorned with beautifully restored Victorian homes. The Trolley Barn once held the trolley cars of the Atlanta and Edgewood Street Railroad Co.

963 Edgewood Ave. N.E.   521-2308
Atlanta
Call for details
Free admission

Kennesaw Mountain National Battlefield Park

Kennesaw Mountain Battlefield marks the location of a critical 1864 engagement in the Civil War. At the visitor's center you will find a small museum with a 10-minute slide show and several exhibits related to the Civil War. During the summer a living history program is presented on Sunday afternoons in the Cheatham Hill area of the park.

Old Highway 41   427-4686
Marietta
8:30 a.m.-5 p.m. daily, weekends 8:30 a.m.-6 p.m.
Free admission

Marietta Square

Antebellum and Victorian homes can be found along the tree-lined streets of Marietta. Enjoy the gardens and park in the Square, spend some time in the restaurants and boutiques or take the walking tour.

4 Depot St.   429-1115
Marietta
Monday-Friday 10 a.m.-4 p.m., Saturday 10 a.m.-3 p.m., Sunday 1-4 p.m.
Free admission

Martin Luther King Jr. Historic District

Visit the King Center and see memorabilia of Dr. King's life and the history of the civil rights movement. Showings of Dr. King's famous speeches on film are 50¢ each. MLK's birthplace is right down the block and the 20-minute free tours are available daily. Ebenezer Baptist Church is on the corner. A self-guided tour map of the entire Preservation District is available free from the National Park Service booth across the street from the MLK Center.

449 Auburn Ave. N.E.   524-1956
Atlanta
May–September 9 a.m.–8 p.m., October–April 9 a.m.–5 p.m.
Free admission

Mauldin Doll Museum

At the Mauldin Doll Museum more than 3,000 dolls and toys are attractively arranged by type—antique dolls, personality dolls, advertising dolls and action dolls. In one room a group of dolls attend a tea party; in another, a lifeguard doll watches over a bathing beauty. Children will delight in searching the museum for their favorite storybook character or TV hero.

2238 Whitfield Place   426-8818
Kennesaw
Tuesday–Saturday 10 a.m.–3 p.m.
Adults, $3; seniors and children, $2

Oakland Cemetery

Established in 1850, Oakland Cemetery is the oldest public cemetery in Atlanta. Buried here under the trees are citizens black and white, gentile and Jew, rich and poor. There are also the graves of six Georgia governors, 23 Atlanta mayors, *Gone With the Wind* author Margaret Mitchell, golf's Bobby Jones and Bishop Wesley Gaines. The 88-acre cemetery is renowned for its stained glass, cast iron, bronzes and Victorian statuary. A visitors center, located inside the cemetery, provides information and offers tours.

248 Oakland Ave. S.E.   577-8163
Atlanta
Monday–Friday 9 a.m.–5 p.m.
Free admission

Rhodes Hall

One of the last of the mansions that once lined Peachtree Street, Rhodes Hall is now the headquarters for the Georgia Trust for Historic Preservation. This 17-room mansion, constructed of Stone Mountain granite in 1903, was modeled after a Bavarian castle. The first floor contains a parlor, reception hall, library, den and dining room and is open to the public.

1516 Peachtree St. N.W.   881-9980
Atlanta
Monday–Friday 9 a.m.–5 p.m.
Adults, $2; children 12 and under, 50¢

Rockdale County Historical Museum

The Rockdale Historical Society maintains its museum in an authentic jailhouse, which was built in 1897. Visitors can see memorabilia from Rockdale County downstairs and tour the jail cells upstairs.

967 Milstead Ave.   922-4326
Conyers
Sundays 3-5 p.m., or by appointment
Free admission

Roswell Historical Society

This mill community, founded in the 1830s, features antebellum homes, churches, historic landmarks and antique and art shops. Walking tour maps are available at the visitor's center.

227 S. Atlanta St.   992-1665
Roswell
Monday-Friday 10 a.m.-4 p.m., closed 1-1:30 p.m.
Donations

Southeastern Railway Museum

The Atlanta Chapter of the National Railway Historical Society maintains this open-air museum featuring more than 40 cars—passenger cars, dining cars, kitchens, cabooses and steam and diesel engines. Twenty to 30 cars are open for inspection, and children will enjoy exploring them. They'll also get a kick out of the steam train and mini-train rides on steam-up weekends.

3966 Buford Highway   476-2013
Duluth
Saturday 9 a.m.–5 p.m.
Free admission

Telephone Museum

Located in the Southern Bell Center, this museum will teach children about the history of the telephone. They'll see early telephones, switchboards, telephone booths and other memorabilia, including a recording of Bell's assistant, Thomas Watson. They will also see how modern satellite communications operate.

675 W. Peachtree St. N.E.   529-7334
Atlanta
Monday–Friday 11 a.m.–1 p.m.
Free admission

The World of Coca-Cola Pavilion

This three-story pavilion adjacent to Underground Atlanta chronicles the development of Coca-Cola, the soft drink that was "born" in Atlanta more than 100 years ago. It features state-of-the-art technology with video touch screens, high definition television, a memorabilia collection and soda fountains serving up your favorite Coke products.

55 Martin Luther King Jr. Drive (Underground Atlanta)   676-5151
Monday-Saturday 10 a.m.-9:30 p.m., Sunday noon-6 p.m.
Adults, $2.50; seniors, $2; children 6-12, $1.50; children under 6, free

Wren's Nest

Children will get a glimpse of Joel Chandler Harris' life as a writer and father when they visit his home. They can see the mailbox in which wrens built a home, giving the house its name, a diorama from "Song of the South," and the bag of string and grumblebox that Harris used to discipline his children. At the end of each tour, visitors can enjoy a tape of one of Harris' Uncle Remus stories. If you visit on Saturday at 2 p.m., you'll be entertained by a storyteller.

1050 Gordon St. S.W.   753-7735
Atlanta
Tuesday-Saturday 10 a.m.-4 p.m., Sunday 1-4 p.m.
Adults, $3; seniors and teens, $2; children 4-12, $1

PARKS AND PLAYGROUNDS

A tlanta has often been referred to as a city in a forest. The stately trees, multitude of greenery, and landscaping enhance this beautiful city that we call "home." And hidden in this great forest are some spectacular and unique parks. As with everything else in Atlanta, there is a great deal of diversity in park facilities. Do a little investigating and exploring to find just the right park for the interests, ages and moods of your family.

Parks and recreational facilities are maintained by counties, as well as local city governments. Listed below are numbers of various parks departments, information about their facilities, as well as highlights of favorite parks and playgrounds where your children can swing, slide, climb and have *fun*!

City of Atlanta

More than 3,000 acres of park land are maintained by the Atlanta Department of Parks, Recreation and Cultural Affairs. This area includes seven regional parks (more than 100 acres), 93 community parks (3-100 acres) and 177 mini-parks (up to three acres). The department operates four indoor pools, 18 outdoor pools, five golf courses, five tennis centers and a variety of recreational, educational and cultural activities at the 39 recreation centers. For more information, call 653-7091.

Grant Park. Just southeast of downtown Atlanta, Grant Park is the home of Zoo Atlanta and its most famous inhabitant, Willie B. The historic Cyclorama is also found there. During the summer, the Atlanta Symphony holds free concerts on the lawn. The open grassy areas, picnic tables and grills make it a popular place for families and large groups. Cherokee Avenue between Sydney Street and Atlanta Avenue.

Piedmont Park. In the heart of Atlanta you will find Piedmont Park, the site of the Arts Festival, Jazz Festival and summer family concerts. In addition to the Botanical Garden, lake, open grassy areas, picnic areas, bench swings and miles of walking paths, children will be delighted with Playscapes. Playscapes is a colorful, sculptured playground that includes a sandbox, giant slide, swings, seesaws and a two-story tower with a circular slide. Piedmont Road between 10th and 13th Streets, Atlanta.

Chastain Park. Chastain Park sits on several acres of rolling hills with shady trees. There are jungle gyms, a wooden playscape with more than 12 stations, toddler swings, regular swingsets, sliding boards and picnic areas. You will also find the Chastain amphitheater, stables, art center, golf course, tennis courts and athletic fields nearby. 234 West Wieuca Road NE, Atlanta.

Neighborhood Parks. Some favorite neighborhood parks in Atlanta with play areas children will enjoy exploring are Garden Hills on Pinetree Drive, Winn Park on Westminister Drive, Adams Park on Delowe Drive and South Bend Park on Compton Drive. Disabled children can enjoy the playground equipment especially designed for them at Anderson Park on Anderson Avenue.

Clayton County

Clayton County Parks and Recreation operates 37 facilities, including three community centers, 29 tennis courts, 13 playgrounds, an equestrian center, two fishing ponds and a nature trail at Reynolds Nature Preserve. Throughout the year they offer courses from quilting to guitar and from cheerleading to drawing. There are also many special events offered each season. For more information, call 477-3766.

Independence Park. Tennis courts, three ball fields, an outdoor basketball court and a covered picnic pavilion are available at Independence Park. Children will enjoy the playground's swings, slides and climbing equipment. 8970 Thomas Road, Jonesboro.

Rex Park. Rex Park has tennis courts, ball fields and picnic areas. There are sandboxes, metal play equipment and wooden structures to entertain little ones. 3499 Rex Road, Rex.

Cobb County

In Cobb County there are 29 park properties, including three pools and four tennis centers. Various sports and recreational programs are available at the Cobb Community Center, Gymnastics Center, Aquatic Center and Ron Anderson Community Center. For more information, call 427-7275.

Terrell Mill Park. Located in East Cobb, Terrell Mill Park offers tennis courts, two covered pavilions, a soccer field, athletic field and large grassy open area for running and kite flying. There are two sets of playground equipment—one is metal and the other is a wooden set with swings, slide and climbing apparatus. Both have a sand base, just right for digging. 480 Terrell Mill Road, Marietta.

Hurt Park. Hurt Park can be found in a heavily wooded area between Austell Road and Hicks Road. There is a large wooden play set with a climbing tower, swinging bridge, poles and slide. A walking track around the soccer field, tennis courts and picnic areas are also available. 990 Hurt Road, Austell.

Larry Bell Park. This park was designed with the special population in mind. There are low beams that make equipment accessible for small children and wheel chairs. In addition to mini-picnic areas, you will find a fitness trail and track. 520 Fairground Street, Marietta.

Decatur

The City of Decatur operates seven parks, including three pools, three ball fields, two sheltered picnic pavilions and tennis courts. The Decatur Recreation Center provides a variety of classes and recreational programs throughout the year. For more information, call 377-0494.

Glenn Lake Park. There's something for everyone in the family at Glenn Lake Park—with a pool, tennis courts, baseball field, soccer field, basketball court, covered pavilion, grills, picnic tables and a creek. There is a tot play area, as well as a school-age structure with slides, swings and climbing equipment. 1121 Church Street, Decatur.

DeKalb County

DeKalb County Recreation and Parks Department maintains 107 parks covering over 3,515 acres. They offer a variety of activities from youth programs to opportunities for the handicapped. There are two golf courses, three tennis centers and 12 pools, in addition to nine recreation centers and 26 youth athletic associations. Within the parks you will find picnic facilities, playground areas, playing fields, lakes and more. For more information, call 371-2631.

Murphey-Candler Park. This 135-acre wooded park provides a lovely retreat any time of year. The park features eight baseball fields, four softball fields, two football fields, tennis courts and a pool. There are also picnic shelters and play equipment scattered around the lake. 1526 West Nancy Creek N.E., Atlanta.

Brookhaven Park. This nine-acre neighborhood park offers a multi-use field, picnic shelter, basketball court and nature trails. There is a well-equipped playground surrounded by trees with crossbars, a slide, tire swings and a platform. 4158 Peachtree Road NE, Atlanta.

Langdale Park. A colorful orange, blue and yellow playground on a sand base awaits you at Langdale Park in South DeKalb. There is a beautiful picnic shelter surrounded by a rock wall, as well as a playing field and multi-use court. 1830 Langdale Drive, Atlanta.

Wade Walker Park. Playing fields, pools and picnic areas are available at Wade Walker Park. There is also an adaptive playground for the disabled. 5585 Rockbridge Road, Stone Mountain.

Fulton County

There are 31 parks covering 2,704 acres under the Fulton County Recreation Department. This area includes 11 community houses, three tennis centers, 90 fields, three lakes, two swimming pools, four gymnasiums and two equestrian centers. For more information, call 730-6200.

Hammond Park. Hammond Park offers tennis courts, picnic shelters, a park center, gym and athletic fields. There are lots of woods for exploring, as well as metal and wood playground equipment with swings, slides, seesaws and climbing areas. 6005 Glenridge Drive, Sandy Springs.

Duncan Park. Residents of South Fulton will enjoy this 143-acre park with its jogging trail, pool, horse rings, community building, shelters and athletic fields. There is a beautiful lake with ducks just waiting to be fed and there are two metal playgrounds. 6500 Rivertown Road, Fairburn.

Chattahoochee River Park. Chattahoochee River Park is one of the best in town for little tykes and older children. The white sand base is great for digging or wiggling your toes in, and there is every wooden play structure imaginable to climb on, slide down, swing on and have fun. The river borders the park and offers a cool breeze, fishing, wading and ducks to feed. Azalea Drive, Roswell.

Gwinnett County

Gwinnett County's 18 parks and recreation spots support a variety of activities, such as picnicking, fishing, fitness trails and hiking trails. Pinckneyville Arts Center promotes cultural activities, and the Lanier Museum offers exhibits on natural history and the cultural history of the county. For more information, call 822-8840.

Best Friend Park. A swimming pool, indoor gym, lighted tennis courts, picnic pavilion and two softball fields are available at Best Friend Park. Get your "best friend" and head for the playground's swings, slides, climbers and giant sandbox. 6224 Jimmy Carter Boulevard, Norcross.

Shorty Howell Park. This park offers a handicap exercise course, fitness trail and large playground in a grassy field. There are also four softball fields, a community building and a lake with ducks. 2750 Pleasant Hill Road, Duluth.

T. W. Briscoe Park. The City of Snellville maintains this well-rounded park which offers something for all age groups. There are ball fields, picnic areas, a pool, wooden playscapes, swings and a small lake for fishing and feeding ducks. 2500 Sawyer Parkway, Snellville.

Marietta

The Marietta Parks and Recreation Department provides a recreational program for all ages with special events throughout the year. Facilities include three recreation centers, a swimming pool, a tennis center, 16 parks and 32 tennis courts. In addition to Glover Park in the center of Marietta Town Square, children will enjoy the following playgrounds. For more information, call 429-4211.

Laurel Park. Little ones love Laurel Park's lake with the ducks that they can feed! There are two metal playground areas with swings, slides and climbing equipment. A walking trail, lighted tennis courts, basketball area, sand volley ball court and large grassy field are other amenities. 151 Manning Road, Marietta.

Wildwood Park. This park offers an interpretative nature trail with signs in both script and Braille, a running loop, challenge-adventure/ropes course and playground structure with a pavilion. Best of all, there are lots of woods to romp in. S. Cobb Drive at Barclay Circle, Marietta.

A. L. Burrus. Here you will find 48 acres with forest, streams and marsh for children to explore. The "latest" in playground equipment can be found next to the picnic pavilion. S. Cobb Drive at U.S. 41, Marietta.

Roswell

The City of Roswell has an active parks and recreation program. Facilities include 11 parks, a pool, tennis courts, a soccer complex and a large community activity center. For more information, call 641-3760.

Roswell Area Park. You'll find a variety of athletic fields, tennis courts, a community activities building, a physical activities center and visual arts center at this 80-acre park in Roswell. For wee ones, there is a fenced-in playground with swings, slides and a sand base. Older children will enjoy the open playground and wooden structures. A family picnic area, jogging/walking trail and lake make this a popular spot all year long. 10495 Woodstock Road, Roswell.

East Roswell Park. Modern playground equipment in bright colors with swings, slides, tubes and climbing apparatus will entertain children at this park. There is also a large picnic shelter and athletic field. Fouts Road and Holcomb Bridge, Roswell.

PARTY! PARTY! PARTY!

Nancy Bennett

O h, no, it's birthday party time again. . .what's a parent to do? Well, it's never a chore in Atlanta to put together a bang-up birthday celebration that your child will remember forever. There are literally hundreds of entertainers who cater to the young set— storytellers, puppeteers, clowns and musicians. Consult this section for these professionals and their specialties, as well as super party places that will handle the entire party for you. Whether you choose one of these facilities or throw the birthday bash at home, there are shops galore to supply you with your party needs— from paper goods to favors. We've listed some of them here for your convenience.

Entertainers

Abracadabra Productions with magician David Marty specializes in children's magical entertainment, balloon animals and fun. 640-5045.

Akbar Imhotep combines storytelling and puppetry, sharing stories from around the world. 688-3376.

Alice Rhodes Puppet Theater performs delightful stories on a professional stage with Standford the Camel and puppet stage manager playing kazoo. 296-7288.

Arts & Crafts Parties lets your child's creativity flow with nine different projects from which to choose. 422-5329.

Arty Parties comes to you with all the art materials for children to make a creative art project to take home. 874-2394.

Beadazzles provides a hassle-free birthday party. Children design and make their own bracelet. 843-8606.

Big Bird II is a big yellow bird who delights your children with games, songs and child participation. 955-1306.

Buttercup and Friends are clowns and storytellers who design theme parties based on a child's interests. Choose from storytelling, magic shows, face painting, cooperative games and balloon animals. 843-0362.

Classy the Clown. Birthday parties, balloons, magic shows, live bunnies and carnival games. 299-5890.

Clownin' Around entertains children of all ages with clown fun. 941-6899.

Entertaining Georgia provides many different types of entertainment: clowns, face painters, spacewalk parties, cotton candy, sno-cone and popcorn machines. Also carnival games, prizes, balloon bouquets and helium rental. 633-8050.

First Step offers dancing parties for boys and girls. Creative movement for ages 3-6, ballet ages 5 and up, aerobic dance for ages 6 and up. 634-0554.

Harry the Hawk, official mascot of the Atlanta Hawks, hands out favors and autographed pictures, does magic tricks and puts on skits at children's parties. 827-3800.

Ima Clown customizes your party with magic, balloon sculptures, face painting, storytelling, buttons and magnets. 879-9286.

Jim Driscoll entertains kids with birthday magic. 996-8009.

Jolly the Clown entertains ages 3-6 with magic, balloon animals, face painting and more. 455-7524.

Jump for Joy has moonwalks available for all party occasions. 962-5690.

Kay's Ponies provides ponies and staff to walk the children around on horseback. Cleanup included. 962-7545.

Kids Can Cook Too! Children ages 3-10 have fun cooking, making candy, decorating ice cream cone cupcakes, decorating the birthday cake and more. Twelve different themes. 231-0524.

Lynnie the Magical Clown. Magic show and balloon sculpturing. 498-6884.

Magic of Jody provides magic, fun and mystery at your party. 482-8158.

Magic Man blends music and comedy into his Oddities Magic Show for Kids. Features friendship rings, Squiggles, Trixter the Live Rabbit and balloon sculptures. 329-0594.

Make Music! offers musical parties for children ages 1-7 with entertainer Jackie Miron. Lots of singing and movement with rhythm instruments, puppets and face painting. 565-6392.

Merry-Go-Round children's parties are theme-related, action-packed with games and prizes. A costumed character tells an imaginative story mixed with fantasy and adventure. 447-7807.

Moonwalk brings fun and excitement to your backyard for an action-packed birthday party. Includes delivery and setup. Rusto Leasing Co. 449-8691.

Mr. Marvel. Family magician featuring Merlin the Rabbit, Mandrake the Bird and Zabo the Clown. 822-1481.

Musical Birthday Parties by singer/guitarist Nancy Kam, who entertains children from 1-12. She teaches songs, uses musical instruments, parachute play, puppets, face painting and more. 378-2919.

Parties by Michelle provides a variety of birthday themes. Decorations, paper goods, favors, cake and costumed characters. 998-3831.

Party Kids has a wide variety of characters and themes to choose from and includes games, activties, entertainment and a bouquet of helium balloons. 664-0022.

Party Pals does parties from setup to cleanup. Professional clowns perform magic, sculpt balloons and paint faces. Theme parties include refreshments, balloons, paper products, loot bags and games. 985-6609.

Peaches and Fufu provides complete entertainment for birthday parties. 498-6400 or 974-8286.

Picadilly Puppets entertains preschoolers with a puppet show full of fantasy and fun. 636-0022.

Pocket People Puppets provides a clown and puppet show to delight children ages 3-6. 455-0210.

Pony Parties provides ponies, staff, to walk the ponies around and cleanup. Seat belts, smiles and favors included. 992-7669.

A Rent-A-Clown provides everything from clowns and costumed characters to jugglers, musicians and face painters. 325-1865.

Rae'ven's Choice Drama Parties provides a birthday story that becomes a play with sets, costumes, props and pantomime along with games, dance, music, balloons and story-telling. 928-4316.

Robots 4 Fun brings a walking, talking, dancing, 4-foot machine, Otto the Robot, to the party. 822-5543.

Sandman Creations sends a sandman to your party where children make sand creations and do sand painting. 457-4870.

Smilemaker's Entertainment provides a fun-filled show by Mr. Fun "The Magical Entertainer" that includes comedy, magic, juggling, puppets and unique balloon animals. 363-9230.

Betty Anne Wylie, storyteller

Stories For All Seasons specializes in birthday parties for ages 3 and up. Betty Ann Wylie spins tales as Coco the Clown, Aunt Betty Bunny and Serena the Fairy Godmother. 355-3951.

Storyteller Cynthia Watts mesmerizes children with her wonderful stories. 758-9873.

T.J. Magical Productions with magician Thomas James and magical clown Jolly Holly makes every child's party magical. 458-3804.

A Tumble Bear Party is an action-filled tumbling class with musical games, gymnastics and sports skills. 448-5437.

Uptown Clown dazzles young and old with his Magical Road Show. Includes magic, balloon sculptures and face painting. 952-1844.

Wallace the Storyteller takes a party of children on a physical and intellectual adventure into familiar literature and includes storytelling, face painting and games. 482-8079.

Wizard of Odd presents birthday magic for kids of all ages. 872-6186.

Zoo Mobile from Zoo Atlanta will come to your party. Choose from four different topics including Georgia Wildlife and Tropical Rainforests. Children will learn some basics about zoology, ask questions and touch small animals. 624-5639.

Party Places

American Adventures birthday parties include pizza, drinks, cake, tokens and tickets. Several party plans to choose from. Cobb Parkway next to White Water, Marietta. 424-9283.

Atlanta Braves offer a sure hit of a birthday party for ages 13 and under. Parties include admission to the game, cake, ice cream, soft drink, souvenirs and more. Kids will meet Rally, Furskin the Bear and Homer the Brave. 522-7630, ext. 383.

Atlanta Music Center's parties bring out the musician in any child. The program uses violins, keyboards, tambourines and other musical instruments. Dunwoody, 394-1727; East Cobb, 977-0003; Lilburn, 979-2887.

Atlanta Scuba and Aquatics Center pool party is splashing fun. Includes pool and party room. 732 Johnson Ferry Road, Marietta. 973-3120.

At'sa Pizza lets the pizza artist in your child loose as he creates his own pizza using different toppings. 3400 Buford Highway. 634-1065.

Ballerina Celebrations for your little ballerina is a special party with costumes, dance and fun designed for children ages 2½ through grade school. 790 Indian Trail, Lilburn. 925-2222.

Brunswick Lanes in Roswell is great fun for older children. Shoe rental, bowling and food are included. 785 Old Roswell Road, Roswell. 998-9437.

Burger King provides food, favors, games, prizes and clean-up. Check local Burger King for more details.

Candy Company offers candy making parties. Children will dip, make candy clusters and other sweet projects. 2550 Sandy Plains Road, Marietta. 973-6468.

Carousel Quarters offers pony rides and petting zoo enjoyment on their Loganville farm or animals and ponies can come to your yard. 466-4670.

Center for Puppetry Arts rents their party room. Includes decorations and tablecloth. Group rates for shows available. 1404 Spring St. 873-3391.

Dance and Arts Showcase offers creative movement, gym and ballet parties for ages 3 and up. Doraville and Lawrenceville. 457-3173.

DeKalb YWCA allows you to rent the entire pool with a lifeguard for children ages 8 and up. Party rooms also available. 2362 Lawrenceville Highway, Decatur. 321-4154.

Double TK Ranch offers pony parties. Parents lead ponies around the ring. 1231 Shallowford Road, Marietta. 926-3795.

Dynamo Swim Center is available for parties, along with a party room. 3119 Shallowford Road, Chamblee. 451-3272.

Fiddlehorse Farm Birthday Parties offers horseback riding, roping, golden horseshoe hunt and petting zoo in a beautiful picnic area. Conyers. 466-1900.

Fire Stations in the metro area often have a small space available where a tour of the station and ice cream and cake can be combined. Policies vary and often depend on the size of the station. Check with your local fire station to see if this service is offered.

First Bounce offers tennis parties with professional instruction and games on child-sized equipment. Atlanta. 698-9622.

Flint Hill Plantation, a recently refurbished antebellum house with columned porches, is available for party rental. 539 S. Peachtree St. Norcross. 263-7669.

Georgia Gymnastics Academy birthday parties provide activities such as trampoline, parachute and deep foam pit with a safety-certified instructor, goodie bags, balloons and paper products. Suwanee, 945-3424; Lawrenceville, 962-5867.

Gwinnett Gymnastics Center supplies gymnastics with an instructor and a party room. Tablecloth, balloons and punch also. 927 Killian Hill Road, Lilburn. 921-5630.

Gymboree celebrates birthdays with parents and children (ages 1-5) with songs, games and activities. Includes special invitations and gift for the birthday child. Three locations: Alpharetta/Roswell, Duluth, Lilburn. 641-0005.

Gym South offers gymnastics parties for children. Fayetteville. 461-3370.

Gym Works provides gymnastics fun with an instructor, setup, cleanup and paper products. Parents and VCRs welcome. 1165 Beaver Ruin Road, Norcross. 925-3636.

It's Magic includes birthday room, play area, adult supervision, maps for guests, drinks and paper products. Additional services available: clowns, magic shows, jugglers, Batman, face painting, goodie bags and more. 292 S. Atlanta St. Roswell. 993-6555.

Kaleidoscope offers T-shirt decorating parties. 2320 Pleasant Hill Road, Duluth. 623-5860.

Karate for Kicks has karate parties with instruction and party fun. 4401 Shallowford Road. 552-8868.

Karate USA party offers exciting and positive atmosphere for children and includes karate lessons plus board breaking demonstration. Duluth, near Gwinnett Place Mall. 587-4306.

Kids in Action provides creative movement and gymnastics at their birthday parties. 4669 Roswell Road N.E., Atlanta. 257-9697.

Lee Wards offers various arts and crafts birthday parties for children. Stone Mountain, 292-6332; Marietta, 564-0872; Morrow, 961-9331.

Lanier Museum of Natural History lets your child celebrate his birthday with games, crafts and old-fashioned fun from the 1800s. Children can dip candles, enjoy hand-churned ice cream and play "old-timey" games. 2601 Buford Dam Road, Buford. 945-3543.

McDonald's birthdays include hamburger, french fries, drink, cake, ice cream, favors and more. Call your local McDonald's for more information.

Mountasia Fantasy Golf offers 18 holes of miniature golf along with everything but the cake. Roswell, 993-7711; Marietta, 422-3440.

Northside YMCA will rent its pool for your party use during its open swim times. A party room is also available. 3424 Roswell Road N.W. 261-3111.

Outdoor Activity Center offers a treasure hunt party in the forest and games for ages 5-10. 1442 Richland Road S.W. 752-5385.

Parkaire Olympic Ice offers parents a worry-free birthday package that includes invitations, drinks, pizza, cake and a skating lesson. Johnson Ferry and Lower Roswell. 973-0753.

Peachtree Road Methodist Church has several party options available: a karate party, gymnastics party, pony party or roller skating party. 3180 Peachtree Road N.E. 266-2386.

Pebble Beach Mini Golf parties are entirely indoors. Parties include pizza, drinks, cookies and 36 holes of mini golf. 4400 Roswell Road N.E., Marietta. 973-7828.

Pirate Cove Miniature Golf has golf and a party deck for birthday celebrations. Venture Parkway at Gwinnett Place Mall, Duluth. 623-4184.

Party Kids

Putt-Putt birthday party packages include a Putt-Putt tournament, video tokens, drinks and cake. Two locations: 3382 Shallowford Road, Chamblee, 458-0888; 4150 Jonesboro Road, Forest Park, 366-7150.

Rainforest Golf parties include 18 holes of golf, use of the party room complete with a jukebox, drinks and paper goods. Open March through November. 5400 Bermuda Road, Stone Mountain. 498-7205.

Red Barn pony parties are held on a petting farm. 800 Rucker Road, Alpharetta. 442-1617.

SciTrek birthday parties include admission to the science museum, party favors and special activities for children ages 5-12. 395 Piedmont Ave. N.E. 522-5500 ext. 12.

Sgt. Singer's makes birthdays special. Birthday packages include cake, tokens, pizza, drinks and special salute from Sgt. Singer. 4649 Memorial Drive. 292-3477.

Show Biz Pizza parties are fun. Pizza, drinks, cake, hats, plates, balloons and tokens are included in the party package. Three locations: Cumberland, 435-9063; Merchants Walk, 971-0002; Norcross, 449-1767.

Skate-A-Long USA parties include admission, skate rental, soda, ice cream, paper products and either pizza or birthday cake. 744 Beaver Ruin Road, Lilburn. 921-0801.

The Soccer Academy's soccer party is sure to delight kids of all ages. A mini-arena is used for kids under 8. Parties include playing time, souvenir cup and more. 327 Arcado Road, Lilburn. 925-4404.

Sparkles Roller Rink party includes admission to the rink, skate rental, party room, cake, soda, party products and decorations. Six locations: Canton, Kennesaw, Marietta, Paulding, Riverdale, Smyrna. 565-8899.

Stone Moutain Park Ice Chalet will take care of everything for a birthday party. Parties include admission, skate rental and skating lesson. Party room, table, tablecloth and balloons also available. Stone Mountain Park parking permit not included. 498-5729.

Swim Atlanta offers birthday parties year-round—for all ages. Includes access to two pools, water toys and party favors. Three locations. 381-7946.

Tolbert-Yilmaz School of Dance birthday parties provide ballet, tap or jazz performance, ballerina parade, games and more. Roswell. 998-0259.

Toy School specializes in preschool birthday parties. Parties include free play, stories, craft cupcakes, ice cream, juice, favor bags and balloon. 55117 Chamblee-Dunwoody Road. 399-5350.

Track of the Pony parties include pony rides and horse games with prizes. Snellville. 932-0108 or 972-1214.

TumbleBears birthday parties are full of fun and fitness. Activities include parachute, tumbling, hoops and balls. Party room available. Buckhead, 266-2386; Gwinnett, 496-0005.

White Water Park's birthday splash party plan includes admission, ice cream novelty, drink in souvenir cup and more. White Water opens in May. Cobb Parkway next to American Adventures, Marietta. 424-9283.

Wildlife Trails at Stone Mountain Park has a rustic cabin to rent for a party. Along with the cabin, an animal handler will bring a small animal up for the children to touch. 498-5603.

Yellow River Game Ranch rents an authentic log cabin. Admission to the park is required, group rates available for 15 or more. 4525 Highway 78, Lilburn. 972-6643.

More Party Stuff

Balloon Barn offers full balloon services, gift cards and party supplies focusing on children's needs. Open seven days per week and offers delivery services. Alpharetta Crossing. 664-4445.

Balloons Over Atlanta/Balloons Over Gwinnett has balloons, helium and balloon decorations (do-it-yourself or professional). Lindbergh Plaza, 231-3090; Stone Mountain Festival, 469-3090.

Bells offers a complete line of party needs for all occasions. Prices range from 5 cents for stuffers to $50 for a unique gift. Six locations. Call 634-5131 for one near you.

Eventz helps to make any occasion special. You do the planning and Eventz does the legwork from a child's birthday party to an intimate dining experience. 378-1146.

Fun Services offers special prices on spacewalks, cotton candy and sno-cone machines. Carnival activities and games are available for parties and school carnivals. Holiday Costume House has children's costumes, makeup and wigs. 1754 Tullie Circle, Atlanta. 321-0049.

One Take Inc. rents high-quality video cameras and accessories for birthdays. Daily, weekend or weekly rental available. 2250 Cobb Parkway, Smyrna. 933-8834.

Paper, Paper, Paper caters to all types of parties with a full line of children's party goods including favors, decorations, games, balloons and paper goods. 263-8210.

Party Station offers more than 40 children's theme patterns and a full line of decorations. They have loot bag fillers, pinatas, balloons, cards and gifts. 5920 Roswell Road, Atlanta. 255-9477.

Party Stuff carries favors, paper goods and party supplies. 977-4511.

P.J. House of Balloons has balloons and gifts for all occasions. Get your birthday supplies here. 642-2110.

You're Invited can provide all your party needs from goodie bag fillers to that special gift. Over 100 balloons and 50 party patterns to choose from. Lawrenceville Town Center. 339-7067.

RESOURCES AND REFERENCES

Help! Fire! Police! How do I register my child for school? Who knows a children's dentist? How do I choose a childcare program for my kids? When you're in a quandary and don't even know where to begin with that "walk through the Yellow Pages," this listing of resources should help. We've included important phone numbers and hotlines, associations serving those with special needs, information on Boy Scouts, Girl Scouts, 4-H and more. We hope parents will find it useful, keep it close to the phone and refer to it often all year long, not just in emergencies!

Childcare

Child Care Solutions 885-1585
   (a Project of Save the Children)
Georgia Child Care Association 483-2408

Education

Public Schools
   Atlanta City 827-8000
   Clayton County 473-2700
   Cobb County 426-3300
   Decatur City 373-5344
   DeKalb County 297-1200
   Fulton County 768-3600
   Gwinnett County 963-8651
   Marietta City 422-3500

Private Schools
   Georgia Department of Education........................... 656-2446

Emergency Numbers

	Fire	Police
Atlanta	911	911
Clayton County	471-4242	471-4242
Cobb County	422-2121	422-5420
DeKalb County	911	911
Fulton County	911	911
Gwinnett County	911	911

Hotlines

Child Find 800-426-5678
Georgia Council on Child Abuse 800-532-3208
"Just Say No" Foundation 800-258-2766
National Center for Missing and Exploited Children 800-843-5678
National Child Abuse Hotline 800-422-4453
National Runaway Switchboard 800-621-4000
Runaway Hotline 800-231-6946

In-Home Childcare and Babysitting

ABC Nannies 512-7702
AuPair Care 800-288-7786
AuPair Homestay USA 262-2049
Freind of the Family 255-2848
Household Personnel Consultants 233-6110
International Household Personnel Consultants 928-7744
Mother's Helping Hand 396-5239
The Nanny Network 252-6512
TLC Sitters of Atlanta 435-6250

Libraries

Libraries are certainly more than they used to be with videos, tapes, special programs, workshops and children's story hour. Call your county for information about the branch nearest you.

Atlanta/Fulton County 730-1700
Clayton Clayton 997-7777
Cobb County 528-2320
DeKalb County 371-3045
Gwinnett County 381-8060

MARTA

The MARTA network of rail stations and buses can get you almost anywhere you want to go in Metro Atlanta for $1.

Information 848-4711

Medical Information

Doctor Referral Service
    Medical Association of Atlanta 881-1714

Dental Referral Service
    Northern District Dental Society 270-1653

Pediatric Hospitals

    Henrietta Egleston Hospital for Children 325-6000
    1405 Clifton Road N.E., Atlanta

    Scottish Rite Children's Medical Center 256-5252
    1001 Johnson Ferry Road, Atlanta

    Cobb General 944-5000
    Kids' Corner provides after-hours pediatric services
    3950 Austell Road, Austell

Tutoring and Educational Services

Homework Help Line
    Atlanta Board of Education 827-8620
    DeKalb Board of Education 939-4951

A-Plus Learning Lab 458-1307
    4330 Georgetown Square, Dunwoody

Audiological Consultants 953-2223
    (two locations)

College Bound–Janet Roskins 452-7074
    (two locations)

Get Smart 664-2825
    265 E. Taylor's Crossing, Alpharetta

Greater Atlanta Speech and Language Clinics 381-1772
    (three locations)

The Learning Place 436-6253
    4200 Paces Ferry Road, Atlanta

Learning Solutions 578-9676
    (five locations)

The Learning Station 255-6700
    4920 Roswell Road, Atlanta

Parents as Teachers 289-5383

Speech Pathology Services 977-7906
    2790 Sandy Plains Road, Marietta

Sylvan Learning Centers of Atlanta 934-6284
    (seven locations)

Visitor Information

Atlanta Chamber of Commerce 880-9000
Atlanta Convention and Visitors Bureau 521-6600
Cobb–Marietta Convention and Visitors Bureau 980-2000
DeKalb Convention and Visitors Bureau 378-2525
Georgia Department of Industry, Trade, Tourism 656-3590
Gwinnett Convention and Visitors Bureau 963-5128
North Fulton Chamber of Commerce and Tourist Commission 993-8806

Youth Clubs and Organizations

Boy Scouts 577-4810

The Boy Scouts of America emphasize citizenship, personal fitness, and character building for boys from first grade through college.

Boys Clubs 527-7100
More than 8,000 boys between 8 and 16 are served by the 12 Boys Clubs in metro Atlanta. Boys Clubs provide a safe environment for learning new leisure skills and making friends.

Camp Fire Girls and Boys 527-7125
Camp Fire is a nationwide organization for boys and girls from kindergarten through high school. Their goal for members is to "learn new skills, gain self-esteem, and give service to their communities."

Girl Scouts 527-7500
The largest volunteer organization for girls in America is the Girl Scouts. Today's Girl Scout program offers opportunities for discovery, growth and community awareness.

Girls Clubs 527-7555
There are six centers around the city where girls can come together to participate in organized activities and educational programs.

4-H
Four-H is the youth development phase of the Georgia Cooperative Extension Service. An emphasis of 4-H is to promote leadership skills and to provide learning experiences in a variety of projects.
Clayton County 473-5450
Cobb County 528-4076
DeKalb County 371-2821
Fulton County 730-7002
Gwinnett County 822-7700

Junior Achievement 257-1932
Junior Achievement helps prepare teens for the world of business with various activities and experiences.

The "Y"
The "Y" provides a wide variety of sports programs, classes, and clubs for boys and girls.
YMCA 588-9622
YWCA 527-7575

Special Services and Support Groups

Everyone needs a little help now and then. You'll surely find it with one of these agencies.

AIDS Atlanta 876-9944

AL-ANON, ALATEEN Family Groups 843-0311

Atlanta Alliance for Healthy Mothers and Children 873-1993
      Referrals for pregnant women and teens

Association for Retarded Citizens of Georgia 761-2745

Atlanta Easter Seal Children's Center 633-9609
      Early intervention programs and therapy and support for children

Better Birth Foundation 469-8870
    Classes in childbirth and infant stimulation

Big Brothers and Sisters 527-7600
    Providing a positive male or female role model for children

Childkind 246-0819
    Support for children with AIDS

Cerebral Palsy United of Georgia 320-6880

Children's Wish Foundation 393-9474
    Granting wishes to terminally ill children

Citizen's Commission on Human Rights 972-9077

Cocaine Anonymous 255-7787

Council for Children Inc. 527-7567
    Advocating legislation and serving as a facilitator with other agencies

Cystic Fibrosis Foundation 325-6973

Diabetes Association 454-8401

Easter Seal Society 633-9609

Epilepsy Foundation 527-7155

Exodus Inc. 873-3979
    Providing alternative educational youth development services for
    the young not successful in regular school

Families in Action 934-6364
    Organization to prevent substance abuse

Families First 853-2800
    Services for abused or neglected children,
    pregnant teens and families in conflict

Family Outreach Center 255-3604
    Telephone counseling, information and referral for individuals and families

FOCUS 483-9845
    For families of children who are chronically or terminally ill

Georgia Council on Child Abuse 870-6565

Georgia Enuresis Control Center 623-8844
    Help for problems with bedwetting

GLRC-Georgia Learning Resource Center
    TheGLRC centers are state-funded programs that provide teaching materials,
    training programs and publications to parents, teachers and agencies
    working with disabled children

Metro East GLRC 325-3011
    2415-C North Druid Hills Road N.E., Atlanta

Metro West GLRC 352-2697
    2268 Adams Drive N.W., Atlanta

LaLeche League 681-6342

Lamaze Childbirth 923-0087
    Information and classes

Lekotek 633-9609
    Parent support group and services for special children

Leukemia Society of America 873-3666

MADD-Mothers Against Drunk Driving........................... 270-9887

March of Dimes Birth Defects Foundation 350-9800
Provides public health education information on prenatal care

Mothers-to-Mothers 320-6667
Support group for expectant and new mothers

Multiple Sclerosis Society 874-9797

Muscular Dystrophy Association 621-9800

Parent to Parent of Georgia 451-5484
Support network linking parents who recently discovered
their child has a disability with experienced parents of a child
with a similar disability

Parents Anonymous 870-6565
Help with parenting and coping skills

Parents Without Partners 590-8552

Spina Bifida Association 972-2885

Sudden Infant Death Syndrome (SIDS)........................ 1-800-541-1783
For parents who child died from SIDS

Tough Love... 250-5100
For parents of troubled teens

Welcome Wagon 955-8770
Information for families new to Atlanta

When Yer Out Ridin' For The Perfect Picture...

...The Trail Ends at Ned Burris Photography

SCIENCE AND NATURE

Yellow River Game Ranch

C hildren have an innate interest in the world around them—the stars, the trees, the animals. Where can they go to observe, question, investigate and learn? Atlanta has some special places that will spark their interest in nature and science, and allow them to explore, learn and have fun—all at the same time! At Fernbank Science Center, they can visit a planetarium, take nature walks, see an authentic space capsule and much more. At the Chattahoochee Nature Center, they can learn about the environment, hike trails and see birds and animals that have been injured and are being "nursed" back to health. Dozens of Atlanta-area parks feature hiking trails and opportunities to view nature firsthand. Why not pack up your budding scientists and nature lovers, and visit one of these spots!

Arabia Mountain

Arabia Mountain is one of the least developed but most accessible granite outcroppings in the Atlanta area. This "mini-mountain," owned by DeKalb County, can be climbed in minutes and offers a beautiful view. Like its neighbors, Stone Mountain and Panola Mountain, Arabia is the toehold for endangered flora that grow only on these outcroppings. A small sign marks the parking lot along Klondike Road. No restrooms.

3850 Klondike Road   371-2631
Lithonia
7 a.m.–sunset
Free admission

Atlanta Botanical Garden

A Japanese garden and sections for roses, herbs and vegetables, plus lovely fountains, make the Botanical Garden a great place to stroll through year-round. In spring its 60 colorful acres are covered with tulips, daffodils, pansies, azaleas, hyacinths and fruit trees. Year-round you will find an oasis of exotic and endangered plants at the Fuqua Conservatory. The garden also offers classes on gardening and flower arranging for adults and children. The visitors center includes an exhibit hall, botanical library and gift shop.

Piedmont Park at South Prado   876-5859
Tuesday–Saturday 9 a.m.–6 p.m., Sunday noon–6 p.m.
Adults, $4.50; children 6–12 and seniors, $2.25
Free admission on Thursdays after 1:30 p.m.

Chattahoochee Nature Center

The Chattahoochee Nature Center features a beautiful selection of trails through 50 acres, and an interpretive center that offers exhibits and classes. Forest walks total one mile and include a treehouse. There is also a ¾-mile boardwalk that winds through the marshes at the edge of the Chattahoochee River. Because of its wildlife rehabilitation program, the center always has some small, wild animals on hand for children to see.

9135 Willeo Road   992-2055
Roswell
9 a.m.–5 p.m. daily
Adults, $2; students and seniors, $1

Chattahoochee River National Recreation Areas

A series of national park lands are strung out along a 48-mile stretch of the Chattahoochee like jewels in a necklace. Each is laced with trails; these range from the hard-surface Cochran Fitness Trail (3 miles)—suitable for joggers, wheelchairs and bicycles—to the muddy foot paths of the Palisades unit, best known to fishermen. The National Park Service has mapped many of these trails; they also sponsor organized excursions.

The Visitors Center has maps of all the trails and other information. Raft rental is for a 2-to-6-hour trip "Shooting the Hooch."

Visitors Center   952-4419 or 394-8335
1978 Island Ford Parkway
Dunwoody
9:30 a.m.–5 p.m. daily

Raft rental-Chattahoochee Outdoor Center   395-6851

Cobb County Petting Farm

Behind the Cobb County Animal Shelter you will find a petting farm. Miss Wiggy, a 900-pound pig, is the star of the barnyard, but she has lots of companions, including goats, chickens, deer, ferrets and sheep. There is also a pond with ducks and geese to feed.

1060 County Farm Drive   499-4136
Marietta
Monday–Friday 9:30 a.m.–5:30 p.m., Saturday 9:30 a.m.–4 p.m.
Reservations only
Free admission

Fernbank Science Center

Fernbank Museum of Natural History

Scheduled to open in late 1991 or early 1992, the Fernbank Museum will feature "A Walk Through Time in Georgia." Visitors will be able to follow the biological, physical and cultural history of Georgia and the Southeast as they learn about science from astronomy to zoology. There will be an IMAX theater, as well as interactive exhibits and graphics where children and adults can investigate and discover at their own level.

1788 Ponce de Leon Ave.   378-0127
Atlanta
Call for additional information

Fernbank Science Center

Fernbank Science Center, operated by the DeKalb County School System and Fernbank Inc., is a learning center for all ages. Year-round the center offers day and evening classes on subjects ranging from planting vegetables to observing constellations. Facilities include an observatory with 36-inch reflecting telescope (largest in the state), planetarium, exhibition hall and greenhouse; outside are gardens and a 70-acre forest with two miles of hard-surface trails as well as a trail with a guide rope and Braille tape recorder for the blind and special trail for those with physical impairments.

156 Heaton Park Drive N.E.   378-4311
Monday 8:30 a.m.-5 p.m., Tuesday-Friday 8:30 a.m.-10 p.m., Saturday 10 a.m.-5 p.m.,
    Sunday 1-5 p.m.
Free admission to science center
Planetarium shows: Adults, $2; children, $1; special children's shows, 50¢

Georgia State Museum of Science and Industry

The fourth floor of the State Capitol offers more than 150 exhibits of mammals, birds, fish, reptiles and much more. The kids won't want to miss the two-headed snake and calf. There is also a fine rock collection, including a moon fragment.

Capitol Hill and Washington Street   656-2844
Monday-Friday 9 a.m.-5:30 p.m., Saturday 10 a.m.-2 p.m., Sunday 1-3 p.m.
Free admission

Kennesaw Mountain National Battlefield Park

This 2,800-acre park offers 16 miles of hiking trails, wooded picnic areas, three recreation fields, 11 miles of earthworks and a museum of Civil War artifacts. A trail meanders one mile from the visitors center to a panoramic view at the top of the mountain.

Old Highway 41   427-4686
Marietta
Visitors center: 8:30 a.m.-5 p.m. daily
Free admission

Lanier Museum of Natural History

The Lanier nature museum offers several wildlife exhibits and an exploration corner where children can handle snake skins, feathers and turtle shells. Outside the museum, follow a nature trail through the museum's botanical garden or climb the 158-foot observation tower. From telescopes in the tower you can see Stone Mountain and Atlanta. Also visit the Bowman-Pirkle House, open Saturday 1-3 p.m., an original 1818 two-story log cabin built by the Cherokee Indians.

2601 Buford Dam Road   945-3543
Buford
Tuesday-Friday noon-5 p.m., Saturday 10 a.m.-5 p.m.
Free admission

\Outdoor Activity Center

The Outdoor Activity Center is Atlanta's only inner-city environmental learning center. Its main attraction is the 26-acre forest with two miles of walking trails around Bush Mountain, a treehouse and playground. There are also guided tours for a small fee.

1442 Richland Road S.W.   752-5385
Sunrise to sunset daily
Free admission

Panola Mountain State Park

This 584-acre park was established to preserve Panola Mountain, a 100-acre granite mass. Hikers have a choice of two self-guided nature trails here: a ¾-mile loop to a granite outcrop and a ¼-mile loop through a micro-watershed. The visitors center offers nature exhibits and workshops that focus on the natural history and ecology of the area.

2600 Highway 155   474-2914
Stockbridge
Tuesday-Friday 9 a.m.-5 p.m., Saturday and Sunday noon-5 p.m.
Free admission

W. H. Reynolds Nature Preserve

This 120-acre preserve offers ponds, streams and a lovely wildlife area. Facilities include an interpretive center with animal displays, picnic areas and four miles of hiking trails.

5665 Reynolds Road   961-9257
Morrow
8:30 a.m.-5:30 p.m. daily
Free admission

SciTrek

The world of physical science is often confusing to children, but SciTrek gives them the opportunity to learn and have fun through hands-on experiences. Learning areas are focused on the principles of color, perception, electricity, magnetism and mechanics. Kidspace is an exciting exhibit for children because they can interact and explore with various materials.

395 Piedmont Ave. N.E.   522-5500
10 a.m.-5 p.m. daily
Adults, $6; children 3-17 and seniors, $4

State Farmer's Market

The State Farmer's Market is the second-largest produce market in the United States. Mounds of fresh fruits and vegetables, a tour of the egg processing plant and a tractor-drawn ride tour of the market are some of the treats waiting for you.

Forest Parkway   366-6910
Forest Park
Open 24 hours, 7 days a week
Tours are given 8:30 a.m.–4:30 p.m. Monday–Friday
Free admission (call in advance for tour)

Stone Mountain Park

Stone Mountain Park is the 3,200-acre home of the world's largest mass of exposed granite and a huge carving. The carving is a memorial to Confederate War heroes Robert E. Lee, Stonewall Jackson and Jefferson Davis. Other attractions include an ice rink, skylift, antebellum mansion, steam-driven locomotive, riverboat, antique auto and music museum, game ranch (with petting area), Civil War exhibits, hiking, tennis, golf, fishing, camping, an inn and restaurants.

Stone Mountain (exit off U.S. 78)   498-5600
Stone Mountain
6 a.m.–midnight daily (attractions operate from 10 a.m.–5:30 p.m., later in summer)
$20 annual vehicle parking permit, $5 daily permit
Most attractions are $2.50, adults; children 3-11, $1.50

Stone Mountain Park Wildlife Trails

At Stone Mountain's Wildlife Trails you can wander along a paved walk and see deer, cougars, elk and bison. There is a pond stocked with wild ducks, and at the Trader's Camp you can feed goats, sheep, rabbits, ponies, chickens and roosters.

Stone Mountain Park   498-5600
Stone Mountain
10 a.m.–8 p.m. daily
Adults, $2.50; children 3-11, $1.50

Swan Woods

Footpaths wind through the 23 acres of Swan Woods, adjacent to the Atlanta History Center. The grounds contain a unique combination of formal gardens and native plant collections.

3101 Andrews Drive N.W.   261-1837
Monday–Saturday 9:30 a.m.–5:30 p.m., Sunday noon–5 p.m.
Adults, $6; children 6-17, $3

Sweetwater Creek State Park

Located 15 miles west of Atlanta, Sweetwater Park offers fishing, boating and picnicking. More than seven miles of trails wind through the park's 2,000 acres of shady hillsides and streams. There are even the ruins of an antebellum factory to be seen.

Route 1, Mt. Vernon Road   944-1700
Lithia Springs
7 a.m.–9:45 p.m. daily
Free admission

Wildwood Park

Wildwood Park provides visitors with 2½ miles of hiking trails, a challenge adventure course, picnic areas and a playground. In addition, there is an environmental study area with concentrated stations for study.

S. Cobb Drive and Barclay Circle   429-4211
Marietta
8:30 a.m.-5:30 p.m. daily
Free admission

Yellow River Game Ranch

The Yellow River Game Ranch is a see-and-touch 24-acre park. Follow the wooded trails to see, pet and feed more than 600 animals, many of which are native to Georgia woods. There are deer, buffalo, bears, mountain lions, foxes, raccoons and other wild and domestic animals. You can buy feed for the animals or bring your own bread, crackers, fruits and vegetables.

4525 Highway 78   972-6643
Lilburn
September-May, 9:30 a.m.-6 p.m.
June-August, 9:30 a.m. till dusk
Adults, $3.50; children 3-11, $2.50

Zoo Atlanta

Zoo Atlanta features more than 900 animals on its 37 acres. You can see the usual lions, monkeys, elephants, rhinos and bears, as well as Willie B. in his new home—the Tropical Rain Forest. Save time for the OK-To-Touch Corral, animal shows in the Wildlife Theater and a ride on the miniature train.

Georgia and Cherokee Avenues, Grant Park   624-5678
Atlanta
10 a.m.-5 p.m. daily
Adults, $6.75; children 3-11, $4

SHOPPING

Ned Burris

n the mall." "Born to shop." "I came, I saw,
till you drop." If you relate to any of these
e this chapter. Whether you're looking for a
ning, an heirloom or a gift, you will certainly find
a's stores. The city boasts huge regional malls,
enters and trendy boutiques. Major department
Rich's, Macy's, J.C. Penney, Sears, Saks Fifth
& Taylor, Neiman-Marcus and others, making
A   hopping "mecca" for residents from around the
South   and visitors from all corners of the globe. Small shops
cater to a variety of tastes and interests, and outlets galore offer
discount prices on everything from cookware to coats. "Happy
shopping!"

Children's Books

One of the best and most long-lasting gifts you can give a child is a book.
Children's Book and Gift Market and My Storyhouse both specialize in
children's books. Bookworms of all ages will find a book that's just right
for them in one of these shops:

B. Dalton, 13 locations, 577-2555

Borders Book Shop, 3655 Roswell Road N.E., Atlanta, 237-0707

Children's Book and Gift Market, 321 Pharr Road N.E., Atlanta, 261-3442

Coles-The Book People, four locations, 476-7410

My Storyhouse, 1401 Johnson Ferry Road (Merchants Festival), 973-2244; 3000 Old
Alabama Road, Alpharetta, 664-8697

Oxford Book Store, 2345 Peachtree Road N.E., Atlanta, 364-2700; 360 Pharr Road, Atlanta,
262-3333

Waldenbooks, nine locations, 297-8865

Waldenkids, Town Center Mall, Kennesaw, 423-0621

Baby Clothing and Equipment

Babies are so cute and cuddly and their arrival is a cause for celebration.
But they also require a whole roomful of furniture and a closetful of
clothes. Check out these stores that specialize in baby items.

Babes and Kids Too, 120 Johnson Ferry Road, Marietta, 565-1420

Baby Biz, Kennesaw, 425-1786; Duluth, 497-1791

Baby Superstore, three locations, 565-2229

Baby's Room, 4281 Roswell Road N.E., Marietta, 565-0892

Bellini Furniture, 736 Johnson Ferry Road N.E., Marietta, 973-7791

Kiddie City, 6285 Roswell Road, Sandy Springs, 252-2904

Lewis of London, 2140 Peachtree Road N.W., 355-1811

New Baby Products, two locations, 321-3874

Kids' Atlanta

Children's Clothing

Never in the history of mankind have children had such a broad and exciting choice in clothing. In addition to the large department stores and chain stores, there are many specialty shops geared just for kids. Most carry clothes for children from birth to teens.

A Razmataz Child, 2391 Peachtree Road, Atlanta, 261-7008

Atlanta Kids, 3655 Roswell Road N.E., 233-1353; 1401 Johnson Ferry Road, Marietta, 565-6667

Brats, 7490 Old National Highway, College Park, 991-3947

Children on Parade, 4282 Highway 78, Lilburn, 979-0260

The Children's Place, four locations, 233-2454

The Children's Shop and the Prep Shop, 2385 Peachtree Road N.E. Atlanta, 365-8496

Chocolate Soup, Phipps Plaza, Atlanta, 261-9672

Finn, Lenox Square, Atlanta, 351-5055

For Crying Out Loud, 3740 Roswell Road N.E. Atlanta, 261-5670

Gap Kids, Perimeter Mall, Atlanta 392-9155

Gretchen's, three locations, West Paces, Dunwoody, Northlake, 237-8020

Kangaroo Pouch, 56 E. Andrews Dr. N.W. Atlanta, 231-1616

Kiddie City, 6285 Roswell Road, Sandy Springs, 252-2904

Kids Kids Kids, 2520 E. Piedmont, Marietta, 977-7496

Kids Mart, five locations, 498-8835

Kids R Us, Kennesaw & Duluth, 623-4208

Little Vickie's Fashions, 7986 Highway 85, Riverdale, 478-8587

The Maypole, 3000 Old Alabama Road, Alpharetta, 664-4426

Mom & Me, 5230 Memorial Dr., Stone Mountain, 296-8045

My Baby & Me, 2141 Roswell Road, Marietta, 977-1778

Petit Mom, 3393 Peachtree Road N.E., Atlanta, 352-2651

Samples Unlimited, Inc., 4373 Roswell Road, Buckhead, 255-6934; 281 S. Main Street, Alpharetta, 664-0207

Small Faces, 1401 Johnson Ferry Road N.E., Marietta, 578-0888

Sprouts, 2100 Roswell Road, Marietta, 565-5577

Sweetpeas, 425 Barrett Parkway, Kennesaw, 424-5152

Village Kids & Their Moms, Vinings, 434-4625

Consignment Shops

"Recycled," "gently worn," "second-hand," are all terms for some of the best deals in town. When kids grow out of clothes every few months, consignment shopping makes sense for budget-minded parents.

Back by Popular Demand, 97 Main Street, Lilburn, 923-2968

Buy Buy Baby, 1670 Lower Roswell Road, Marietta, 977-4641

Clothes Hanger, 484 Norcross-Tucker Road, Norcross, 446-7052

Consignment Unlimited, 1950 Canton Road, Marietta, 427-0806

Cute Kids, 8142 Highway 85, Riverdale, 477-5144

Deja Vu, 112 Norcorss Street, Roswell, 998-2308

Fabulous Finds, 2334 Main Street, Tucker, 723-0143

Finders Keepers, 116 N. Avondale Road, Avondale Estates, 296-0285; 4282 Highway 78, Lilburn, 979-7346

Glad Rags, 9850 Nesbit Ferry Road, Alpharetta, 992-3134

Hand-Me-Ups, 768 Concord Road S.E., Smyrna, 435-6202; 4448 Marietta Street S.W., Powder Springs, 439-8200

Just 4 Kids, 5350 Peachtree Road, Chamblee, 451-0533

My Sister's Closet, 5352 Peachtree Road, Chamblee, 458-8362

New-To-You, 359 West Shadburn Ave., Buford, 945-5930

Our Family Closet, 3098 Buford Highway, Duluth, 476-7974

Play It Again, 273 Buckhead Ave., Atlanta, 261-2135

Play It Again, Sam, 6375 Spaulding Dr., #E, Norcross, 446-6153

Replay, 290 Hilderbrand Dr. N.E., Sandy Springs, 843-1080

ReRuns, 1066 Canton Street, Roswell, 992-6711; 2518 Piedmont Road N.E., Marietta, 565-0121; 79 S. Main Street, Alpharetta, 664-1705

Saraja's, Inc., 3101 Roswell Road N.E., Marietta, 565-1447

Second Hand Rose, 1260 N. Highway 85, Fayetteville, 461-5160

The Second Time Around, 4813 Rockbridge Road, Stone Mountain, 292-8426

Second Debut, 1297 Roswell Road N.E., Marietta, 971-2804

Something Old, Something New, 4489 Bells Ferry Road N.W., Marietta, 591-1122

Sweet Repeats, 3181 Roswell Road N.E., 261-7519

Costumes

Halloween is not the only time of year that kids need costumes. School plays, book reports and birthday parties are other times kids might need a quick change.

Atlanta Costume, two locations, 874-7511

Costume Architects, 1536 Monroe Dr. N.E., Atlanta, 875-6275

Costume Crafters, 2979 Peachtree Road N.E., 237-8641

Dance Fashions, 10390 Alpharetta Street, Roswell, 998-0002

Eddie's Trick Shop, three locations, 296-5653

Holiday Costume, 1754 Tullie Circle N.E., 321-0049

Taffy's, 318 E. Paces Ferry Road N.E., 261-3670

Educational/Learning Materials

If your child needs extra help at home or you'd like to give a "toy" that will help him learn or you're a teacher looking for supplies, check out these stores. These specialized businesses have just what you need when it comes to educational and learning materials.

A to Z Parent Teacher Center, 2391 Beverly Hills Dr., Chamblee, 458-5377

ABC School Supply, Inc., 3312 N. Berkley Lake Road, Duluth, 497-1516; Toco Hills Shopping Center, 636-6635

Academic Software (educational software and computers), 10479 Alpharetta Street, Roswell, 998-7766.

Atlanta Toy and School Supply, Inc., 384 Ralph McGill Blvd., 525-0551

Early Learning Center, four locations, 698-8760

Educational Record Center (records, tapes and videos), 1575 Northside Dr. N.W., 352-8282

Hammett Learning World, 5920 Roswell Road N.W., 257-1005

J&R Educational Supplies, 1489 Roswell Road, Marietta, 565-4889

Learning World, 3965 Rockbridge Road, Stone Mountain, 292-4236; 4865 Jonesboro Road, Forest Park, 366-7767

School Tools and Office Pals, Inc., 2706 Mountain Industrial Blvd., Tucker, 270-1828

Stevens Educational Curriculum, 3427 Oakcliff Road, Doraville, 455-4640

Teacher's Place, 31 Atlanta Street S.E., Marietta, 427-7361

Furniture For Children

Buying furniture for a baby or child is certainly a major purchase. From cribs to beds that look like fire trucks, from simple pictures to walls that look like a scene from Star Wars—you'll find it all at one of these locations.

Babes and Kids Too, 1205 Johnson Ferry Road, Marietta, 565-1420

Baby Biz, Outlets Ltd. Mall in Kennesaw and Duluth, 425-1786

The Baby's Room, 4281 Roswell Road, Marietta, 565-0892

Baby Superstore, three locations, 565-2229

Bellini Furniture, 736 Johnson Ferry Road N.E., Marietta, 973-7791

Cocoon Home Furnishings, Olde Mill Shopping Center, Marietta, 971-7592

Kids Furniture World, 6508 Dawson Blvd., Norcross, 449-5960

Lewis of London, 2140 Peachtree Road N.W., 355-1811

New Baby Products, 2200 Cheshire Bridge Road N.E., Atlanta, 321-3874; 5050 Jimmy Carter Blvd., Norcross, 449-8970

Solid Pine USA, three locations, 591-8584

Miscellaneous Shops & Services
Decorating

Kids' rooms don't have to be a mess. These businesses will help you decorate and organize your child's room.

Child's Play, 261-2924

Karen's Fabrics, 969 Canton Street, Roswell, 587-5352

Hair Styling

Getting a child's hair cut is often traumatizing for both parent and child. Visit one of these salons that specialize in kid's cuts.

Kids Kuts, 6011-A Memorial Dr., Stone Mountain, 498-1171

Kid's Kuts, 3000 Old Alabama Road, Alpharetta, 664-9506

Kuts for Kids, Ltd., Kroger Center, Highway 78, Snellville, 979-5800

Playground Equipment

Children are "naturals" when it comes to swinging, sliding, climbing and hanging. You can get a simple rope swing or an elaborate play structure that will bethe envy of the neighborhood at one of these locations.

Creative Playthings, 6332 Warren Dr., Norcross, 448-3475

Great American Swing Company, 7380 Roswell Road, Sandy Springs, 551-9535

King of Swings, I-85 at Indian Trail, Norcross, 448-5464

Plantation Playgrounds, Carrollton Highway, Newnan, 1-404-251-1527

Redwood Designs, 3000 Canton Road N.E., Marietta, 421-9023

Superior Playsets, Inc., Acworth, 928-6744

Yards of Fun, 4313 Northeast Expressway Access Road, Doraville, 939-5040

Toys

A visit to one of these toy stores will have you wishing you were a child again. It's fun to look, wish and dream!

Atlanta Doll, 1054 Lindbergh Dr. N.E., Atlanta, 248-1151

The Children's Hour, Second and Manor Dr., Stone Mountain Village, 498-1351

Circus World, six locations, 432-1281

Cottage Doll Shop, 2409 E. Main St., Snellville, 985-0435

Discovery Toys, 636-4648; 633-1158

Dolls 'N Gifts, 3500 Gwinnett Place Dr., Duluth, 623-9525

Early Learning Centre, four locations, 698-8760

Elizabeth's Dollhouse, 164 W. Wieuca Road N.W., Atlanta, 256-4288

Embraceable Zoo, five locations, Kennesaw, Gwinnett Place, Northlake, Perimeter and Southlake, 399-6444

F.A.O. Schwarz, Lenox Square, Atlanta, 233-8241

Kay-Bee Toy and Hobby, three locations, 476-9515

Kiddie City, 6285 Roswell Road, Sandy Springs, 252-2904

Lenox Toys and Hobbies, Lenox Square, Atlanta, 237-6371

Learning Toys, 10800 Alpharetta Highway, Roswell, 594-8968

Lionel Play World, six locations, 292-5003

Toy Box, 231 Peachtree Street N.E., Atlanta, 524-1304

The Toy School, 5517 Chamblee Dunwoody Road, Dunwoody, 399-5350

The Toy Store at Ansley Mall, 1544 Piedmont Ave. N.E., Atlanta, 875-1137

Toy Trains 'N Things, 5095-B Buford Highway, Doraville, 452-0856

Toys 'R' Us, five locations, Atlanta, Tucker, Duluth, Decatur and Morrow, 951-8052

The Village Doll Shoppe, 907 S. Main Street, Stone Mountain Village, 498-7400

SPORTS AND RECREATION

Stephen Davis

B ecause of its temperate weather, Atlanta is a paradise for sports enthusiasts of all ages. Youth organizations around the city offer highly structured programs for children and young people year-round—in soccer, football, baseball and basketball. For those interested in tennis, karate, gymnastics or golf, there are classes available throughout the year. Choose a private instructor or school, a county recreation department or a church program— whatever your pocketbook allows. Consult this comprehensive listing, as well as Atlanta Parent newspaper, for the activity or sport that appeals to your child.

Baseball

Baseball has come a long way from the sand lots our grandparents played in long ago. However, despite the fancy uniforms and metal bats, the excitement at the baseball diamond has changed very little over the years. In addition to recreation departments and churches, these community organizations have league teams for boys and girls of all ages:

Briarcliff Community Sports, 1400 McConnell Drive, Decatur, 634-8055

Clairmont Youth Sports, 2295 Dresden Drive, Chamblee, 321-9085

Forest Park Athletic Association, South Avenue, Forest Park, 363-2157

Lilburn Dixie Baseball, Lions Club Drive, Lilburn, 381-7510

Murphey-Candler Little League, E. Nancy Creek Drive, Chamblee, 429-4211

Norcross Youth Athletic Association, 211 N. Cemetery St. N.W., Norcross, 840-8126

Northside Youth Organization, 20 W. Wieuca Road N.E., Atlanta, 256-1483

Redan Athletic Association, Phillips Road, Lithonia, 484-1109

Sandy Springs Youth Sports, Morgan Falls Road, Dunwoody, 396-0330

Basketball

Interest in basketball has grown rapidly in the South in the past 20 years. If there is a basketball gym near you, chances are they will have a youth basketball league. Refer to the list of recreation departments, churches and the "Y" in this chapter for phone numbers.

Bicycling

The Southern Bicycle League sponsors tours and bike rides throughout the year.

Southern Bicycle League, 320-7239 or 594-8350

Bowling

Check with the bowling lanes nearest you to find out about lessons and children's leagues or call:

Greater Atlanta Bowling Association   872-2896
756 W. Peachtree Street N.W.

Church Leagues

Many churches in the Atlanta area sponsor sports leagues and athletic programs throughout the year, including soccer, basketball and baseball.

Briarlake Baptist   325-4214
3715 Lavista Road, Decatur

Dunwoody Baptist   394-6275
1445 Mount Vernon Road, Dunwoody

Jewish Community Center Zaban Park   396-3250
5342 Tilly Mill Road, Dunwoody

Peachtree Road United Methodist   266-2386
3180 Peachtree Road N.E., Atlanta

Peachtree Presbyterian   842-5800
3434 Roswell Road N.W., Atlanta

Rehoboth Baptist   939-4603
2997 Lawrenceville Highway, Tucker

Fencing

Whether you have a budding Sir Lancelot or Joan of Arc, fencing will provide a good workout, sharpen coordination and balance and add a dash of romance to your child's life.

Atlanta Fencer's Club   892-0307
40 7th Street N.E.

Fishing

Fishing is a wonderful activity that children can enjoy with their parents and grandparents. Georgia is "brimming" with lakes and streams for you to try your luck, but first, get a license!

Georgia Game and Fish Division   493-5770

No license is required at these private lakes.

Browne's Lake   No phone
Pleasant Hill Road
Lilburn

Cedar Grove Lakes   964-3001
6285 Cedar Grove Road
Fairburn

DeMooney Lakes   964-1789
4070 DeMooney Road
College Park

Lake Carlton
466-4829
3552 Lake Carlton Road
Loganville

Rainbow Ranch   1-404-887-4797
Highway 20
Cumming

Twin Brothers Lake   496-0002
3546 Stapp Drive
Tucker

Football

Georgians have always been partial to football, and your child doesn't have to wait until high school to begin to play. In addition to recreation departments and community organizations previously listed, your child can register for football at:

Greater Lilburn Athletic Association   923-8473
Lions Club Drive, Lilburn

Gresham Park Youth Football   244-9600 or 244-9660
3113 Gresham Road S.E., Atlanta

Golf

Private clubs and public golf courses provide youngsters with the opportunity to play golf and take lessons. The more serious golfer should contact:

Atlanta Junior Golf Association   355-9472
384 Woodward Way, Atlanta

Georgia Junior Golf Foundation   233-4742
4200 Northside Parkway, Atlanta

Gymnastics

The Olympics have certainly sparked interest in gymnastics in recent years. There is a broad range of gymnastics instruction available from those for parents and infants to highly competitive teams.

ABC in Motion
925-2222
790 Indian Trail Road
Lilburn

Academy of Sports
981-8000
5020 Snapfinger Woods Dr.
Decatur

Atlanta School of Gymnastics
938-1212
3345 Montreal Station
Tucker

Chattooga School of Gymnastics
924-2832
4005 Highway 5
Marietta

Fantastic Gymnastics
623-8211
3585 Peachtree Industrial
Duluth

Georgia Gymnastics Academy
(2 locations)
962-5867
84 Patterson Road
Lawrenceville

945-3424
50 Old Peachtree Road N.E.
Suwanee

Gym South School of Gymnastics
461-5528
119 N. 85 Parkway
Fayetteville

Gymboree
641-7029
East Cobb, North Atlanta, Roswell

Gymboree
641-0005
Alpharetta, Roswell, Duluth, Lilburn

Gymset
971-0060
4957 Lower Roswell Road N.E.
Marietta

Gym Works
925-3636
1165 Beaver Ruin Road
Norcross

Kid Nastics
448-5437
5270 Peachtree Parkway
Norcross

Kids in Action
257-9697
175 Mt. Vernon Highway N.E.
Sandy Springs

Gwinnett Gymnastic Center
921-5630
927 Killian Road
Lilburn

Lawrenceville School of Gymnastics and Dance
995-9930
508 Grayson Highway
Lawrenceville

Gym America Gymnastics
491-0088
4679 Hugh Howell Road
Tucker

Rockdale Gymnastics
483-0229
1774 Old Covington Road
Conyers

Gym Elite
448-1586
6670 Jones Mill Court
Norcross

Tumble Bears
266-2386
Buckhead

Horseback Riding

Children progress from their hobby horses and stick ponies to wanting to ride the "real thing." What child wouldn't be enthusiastic about riding a horse or pony at one of these stables?

Briarcliff Stables
475-4761
885 Mullinax Road
Alpharetta

Pounds Stables
394-8288
7910 Nesbit Ferry Road
Doraville

Chastain Stables
257-1470
4371 Powers Ferry Road N.W.
Atlanta

Rocky Pine Ranch
926-3795
1231 Shallowford Road N.E.
Marietta

Fox Hollow Farms
971-3437
3556 Robinson Road
Marietta

Sweet Sunshine Farm
475-8319
14675 Thompson Road
Alpharetta

Huntcliff Stables
993-8448
9072 River Run Road
Dunwoody

Track of the Pony
932-0108

Linda's Riding School
922-0184
3475 Daniels Bridge Road
Conyers

Vogt Riding Academy
321-9506
1084 Houston Mill Road N.E.
Atlanta

Ninebarks Stables Riding Center
476-1356
412 Kemp Road
Suwanee

Wills Equestrian Center
475-3470
11915 Wills Road
Alpharetta

Ice Skating

Although Atlanta's weather is seldom cold enough to freeze a pond, the following rinks do offer year-round ice skating and lessons for children:

Parkaire Olympic Ice Arena   973-0753
4880 Lower Roswell Road N.E., Marietta

Ice Chalet   498-5729
Georgia's Stone Mountain Park, Stone Mountain

The rink at Parkaire also has hockey teams for children.

Karate

In addition to what karate does for the body, it teaches self-discipline and helps children improve their self-concept.

All American Karate Joe Corley Studios (6 locations)   252-8200

Karate USA (3 locations)   587-4306
Roswell, Duluth and Alpharetta

Kim Brothers Karate (8 locations)   498-9900

Miniature Golf

American Adventures   424-9283
250 N. Cobb Parkway, Marietta

Mountasia Fantasy Golf   993-7711 or 422-3440
Roswell and Marietta

Pebble Beach Mini Golf   973-7828
4400 Roswell Road N.E., Marietta

Pirate Cove Adventure Golf   623-4184
3380 Venture Parkway, Duluth

Putt Putt Golf & Games
Chamblee   458-0888
Forest Park   366-7150
Marietta   422-7997

Rainforest Golf   498-7205
5500 Bermuda Road S.W., Stone Mountain

Recreation World   339-1400
1100 Highway 120, Lawrenceville

Polo

Not only the rich and famous need enjoy polo. You can watch it Sunday afternoons from June through October at the following fields:

Atlanta S.E. Polo Club   688-7656
Cumming

Southeastern Polo Club   659-5701
Highway 371, South Forsyth County

Rafting

Whether you like a leisurely afternoon floating down the Chattahoochee or the excitement of white water rapids, you're within reach of both:

Atlanta White Water Club   299-3752

Chattahoochee Raft and Canoe Rental   998-7778
199 Azalea Drive, Roswell

Chattahoochee Outdoor Center   395-6851
1990 Island Ford Parkway, Dunwoody

Southeastern Expeditions   329-0433
2936-H N. Druid Hills Road, Atlanta

Roller Skating

All American Skating Center
469-9775
5400 Bermuda Road
Stone Mountain

Golden Glide Skateport
288-7773
2750 Wesley Chapel Road
Decatur

Jellibeans
346-1111
3850 Stone Road S.W.
Atlanta

Old Dixie Roller Rink
363-9613
262 Johnson Road
Forest Park

Rainbow Roller Rink
981-3121
5480 Browns Mill Road
Lithonia

Roswell Roller Rink
998-9700
780 Old Roswell Road
Roswell

Screaming Wheels Roller Rink
752-5597
1724 Stewart Ave. S.W.
Atlanta

Skate–A–Long USA
921-0800
744 Beaver Ruin Road
Lilburn

Skate Palace
961-5110
6766 Mt. Zion Blvd.
Morrow

Skate Town South
768-0095
5570 Old National Highway
College Park

Sparkles Roller Rinks
565-8899
5 locations

Stone Mountain Park Trailskate
498-5600
Stone Mountain

Skiing

Ski experts say, "The younger the better." You can find out about lessons and nearby slopes by calling:

Atlanta Ski Club   255-4800
6303 Barfield Road, Atlanta

Soccer

The fact that most children know more about soccer than their parents do suggests the tremendous popularity that this sport has achieved in the past 10 years. All over the city you will find league teams in the fall and spring for boys and girls of all ages. Many organizations even have winter indoor soccer teams. Churches, recreation departments, the "Y" and community organizations will probably have a place for your child. For additional information call:

Georgia State Soccer Association   452-0505
3684 Stewart Road, Doraville

The Soccer Academy   925-4404
327 Arcado Road
Lilburn

Special Olympics

Georgia Special Olympics is a wonderful organization for parents and children with special needs to get involved in:

Georgia Special Olympics   458-3838
3166 Chestnut Drive, Doraville

Michelle Brown

Swimming

What do guppies, whales and children have in common? They all love to swim. But swimming is no longer limited to the summer months, with many year–round pools available in the Atlanta area.

Indoor

Dynamo Swim Center
451-3272
3119 Shallowford Road
Chamblee

Swim Atlanta
992-7946
Roswell, Lilburn and N.W. Atlanta

Clarence Duncan Park Pool
964-7800
6000 Rivertown Road
Fairburn

Mountain Park Pool
925-0047
5050 Five Forks Trickum Road
Lilburn

Cobb County Aquatic Center
422-4457
520 Fairground Street
Marietta

M. L. King South Pool
658-6099
582 Connally Street
Atlanta

M. L. King North Pool
688-3791
70 Boulevard
Atlanta

J. F. Kennedy Pool
588-0839
225 James P. Brawley Drive S.W.
Atlanta

Perry Homes Pool
794-0161
Perry Blvd.
Atlanta

Outdoor Pools

City of Atlanta

Adams Park
753-6091
1581 Lagoon Drive
Atlanta

Candler Park
373-4349
1500 McLendon Ave. N.E.
Atlanta

Chastain Park
255-0863
235 W. Wieuca Road N.W.
Atlanta

Garden Hills Park
233-2753
335 Pinetree Drive
Atlanta

Grant Park
622-3041
625 Park Ave. S.E.
Atlanta

Piedmont Park
892-0117
Piedmont Ave. @ 14th Street
Atlanta

Gresham
243-9904
3113 Gresham Road S.E.
Atlanta

Joyland Park
622-3043
1616 Joyland Place
Atlanta

Oakland Park
753-7245
1305 Oakland Drive
Atlanta

Powell Park
753-7156
1690 Martin Luther King, Jr. Drive
Atlanta

Maddox Park
892-0119
1142 Bankhead Ave.
Atlanta

DeKalb County

Briarwood
321-9500
2235 Briarwood Way N.E.
Atlanta

Ebster Pool
378-4303
440 W. Trinity Place
Decatur

Glen Lake Pool
378-7671
1121 Church Street
Decatur

Kittredge
321-9700
2353 N. Druid Hills Road
Atlanta

Lithonia Pool
482-9915
6718 Parkway Road
Lithonia

Lynwood Pool
255-9820
3360 Osborne Road
Atlanta

Mark Trail Pool
241-9023
2230 Tilson Road
Decatur

Medlock Pool
321-9861
854 Gaylemont Circle
Decatur

Midway
289-9709
3181 Midway Road
Decatur

Murphey Candler Pool
455-9702
1526 W. Nancy Creek Road
Chamblee

DeKalb County

Tobie Grant
299-9911
644 Parkdale Drive
Scottdale

Kelley C. Cofer (Tucker Pool)
491-9718
4257 N. Park Drive
Tucker

Wade Walker Pool
469-9163
5585 Rockbridge Road
Stone Mountain

Gwinnett County

Best Friends Park Pool
447-0032
6224 Jimmy Carter Blvd.
Norcross

Briscoe Park Pool
972-6072
2500 Sawyer Parkway
Snellville

Dacula Park Pool
962-7309
205 Dacula Road
Dacula

Clayton County

Clayton County Pool
478-1271
1535 Flicker Road
Jonesboro

Cobb County

King Springs Park Pool
431-2844
3530 King Springs Road S.E.
Smyrna

Fulton County

Delano Park Pool
762-6708
4730 Bailey Street
College Park

Tennis

If you say, "Tennis anyone?" around Atlanta, you'll hear a resounding, "You bet!" There are leagues available for beginners to professionals from the age of 8 on up through the Atlanta Lawn Tennis Association. Lessons for children as young as 2½ are offered at Dunwoody Tennis School's "Tennis for Tykes" program. Lessons and clinics are also sponsored at various public and private courts throughout the metro area.

Atlanta Lawn Tennis Association (ALTA)
399-5788
1140 Hammond Drive N.E.
Atlanta

Bitsy Grant Tennis Center
351-2774
2125 Northside Drive N.W.
Atlanta

Blackburn Tennis Center
451-1061
3501 Ashford Dunwoody Road N.E.
Atlanta

Burdett Tennis Center
996-3502
5975 Old Carriage Drive
College Park

DeKalb Tennis Center
325-2520
1400 McConnell Drive
Decatur

Harrison Park Tennis Center
591-4545
2650 Shallowford Road N.E.
Atlanta

Kennworth Park Tennis Center
974-9515
Highway 293 N.W.
Acworth

North Fulton Tennis Center
256-2377
500 Abernathy Road N.E.
Atlanta

Pleasant Hill Park Tennis Center
476-5505
3620 Pleasant Hill Road N.W.
Duluth

Roswell Tennis Center
641-3775
Woodstock Road
Roswell

Dunwoody Tennis School–Ty Fuller
394-0387
1165 Spalding Drive
Dunwoody

South Fulton Tennis Center
964-1388
5645 Mason Road
College Park

Fair Oaks Tennis Center
424-0204
1460 Brandon Drive S.W.
Marietta

Sweetwater Park Tennis Center
944-3938
2447 Clay Road S.W.
Austell

The First Bounce
698-9622
Sandy Springs, E. Cobb

Terrell Mill Park Tennis Center
952-6076
480 Terrell Mill Road S.E.
Marietta

Atlanta Track Club

Track

Children are natural runners and will enjoy participating in local fun runs held throughout the metro area. The Junior Peachtree (held the first Saturday in June) and All Comers Track Meets (children and adults) are two events open to children during the summer months. The Atlanta Streakers is a youth track and cross country team for boys and girls ages 6-14. They practice at Lakeside High School and participate in state, regional and national meets.

Atlanta Track Club   231-9064
3097 E. Shadowlawn Ave. N.E., Atlanta

Walking and Hiking

From the time your child is born, walking is an activity that can be mutually enjoyable for both of you. One of the benefits of Atlanta's weather is that you can enjoy walking all year long. There are birds to entertain you in the spring, crickets in the summer, crunching leaves in the autumn and stillness in the winter. Explore your neighborhood, parks, nature centers, or call the Appalachian Trail Club to really broaden your horizons.

Atlanta Botanical Garden
876-5858
Piedmont Park
Atlanta

Arabia Mountain
371-2548
3850 Klondike Road
Lithonia

Chattahoochee Nature Center
992-2055
9135 Willeo Road
Roswell

Chattahoochee River Recreation Area
952-4419
1900 Northridge Road
Roswell

Fernbank Science Center
378-4311
156 Heaton Park Drive N.E.
Atlanta

Oakland Cemetery
577-8163
248 Oakland Ave. S.E.
Atlanta

Outdoor Activity Center
752-5385
1401 Bridges Ave. S.W.
Atlanta

Panola Mountain State Park
474-2914
2600 Highway 155
Stockbridge

Reynolds Nature Preserve
961-9257
5665 Reynolds Road
Morrow

Stone Mountain Park
498-5600
Stone Mountain

Swan Woods
Atlanta History Center
261-1837
3101 Andrews Drive N.W.
Atlanta

Sweetwater State Creek Park
944-1700
Mt. Vernon Road
Lithia Springs

Wildwood Park
429-4211
S. Cobb and Barclay Circle
Marietta

Parks and Recreation Departments

County and city recreation departments sponsor a broad range of athletic and recreational teams and programs for children. Most publish a quarterly brochure that lists activities and special events and they will be glad to send you a copy.

Atlanta Parks, Recreation and Cultural Affairs, 653-7091

Alpharetta Recreation Department, 442-0105

Clayton County Parks and Recreation, Jonesboro, 477-3766

Cobb County Parks and Recreation, Marietta, 427-7275

College Park Recreation Department, 669-3767

Decatur Parks and Recreation, 377-0494

DeKalb County Recreation, Parks and Cultural Affairs, Decatur, 371-2631

Douglasville Parks and Recreation, 920-3007

East Point Recreation Department, 765-1082

Forest Park Recreation Department, 363-2908

Fulton County Parks and Recreation, Atlanta, 730-6200

Gwinnett County Parks and Recreation, Lawrenceville, 822-8840

Hapeville Recreation Department, 669-2136

Kennesaw Parks and Recreation, 422-9714

Lawrenceville Recreation Department, 963-3510

Marietta Parks and Recreation, 429-4211

Roswell Recreation and Parks, 641-3760

Smyrna Parks and Recreation, 434-6600

Snellville Recreation and Parks, 972-1677

Georgia State Soccer Association

"Y" Programs

The YMCA and YWCA continue to take an active role in providing sports and recreation for Atlanta's youth:

Metropolitan YMCA (12 locations)   588-9622
100 Edgewood Ave. N.E., Atlanta

Metropolitan YWCA (5 locations)   527-7575
100 Edgewood Ave. N.E., Atlanta

Spectator Sports–Professional

The inspiration for most children's sports participation springs from watching professional and college athletes. In Atlanta, win or lose, indoors or outdoors, sports fans can root for teams all year.

Kids' Atlanta

Atlanta/Fulton County Stadium, 521 Capitol Ave. S.E., and the Omni Coliseum, 100 Techwood Drive are the home fields for the teams.

Atlanta "Attack" Soccer, 2859 Paces Ferry Road, Suite 830, Atlanta, 431-6111

Atlanta Braves Baseball, 521 Capitol Ave. S.E., Atlanta. Baseball club, 522-7630, or ticket office, 577-9100.

Atlanta Falcons Football, I-85 and Suwanee Road, Suwanee, 945-1111. Ticket office, 950 East Paces Ferry Road N.E., 261-5400.

Atlanta Hawks Basketball, 100 Techwood Drive N.W., 827-3800.

Spectator Sports-College

The Georgia Tech Yellow Jackets and Georgia State Panthers also call Atlanta "home." In addition to Georgia Tech and Georgia State, Atlanta University, Emory, Kennesaw and many other colleges and universities sponsor athletic programs that children would enjoy.

Atlanta University, 522-8980

Emory, 727-6123

Georgia Tech, Grant Field, 894-5447

Georgia State, Sports Information, 651-2772

Kennesaw, 423-6000

Oglethorpe University, Sports Information, 261-1441

University of Georgia, Sports Information, 1-542-1231

TOURS

Georgia Department of Industry, Trade and Tourism

Georgia State Capitol

T aking a tour with children is like walking through the pages of a book where page comes alive. What an exciting way to learn about our past, present and future. . .about manufacturing. . .careers. . .science and much, much more. Rule #1 in taking a tour is to *call ahead* to schedule your trip and get specific details about group size, times, age restrictions, etc. In addition to the tours listed in this chapter, many of the museums, attractions and historical sites listed in other sections of this book offer guided tours.

Airports

Atlanta-Hartsfield International Airport

A visit to the Atlanta Airport is like a trip into some future time zone. Explore the moving sidewalks, trams and concourses on your own or call Delta Airlines (765-2600) to schedule a guided tour of a plane.

Atlanta Hartsfield Airport   530-6600
Hapeville

State Hanger at Fulton County Airport/Charlie Brown Field

Call to reserve a tour of the official state hanger. Tours include the inside of an airplane and maybe a glimpse of the governor's or lieutenant governor's plane. Children must be 5 years old and groups should be limited to 20.

4175 South Airport Road   699-4483
Atlanta

DeKalb-Peachtree Airport

Check out their observation deck where families can watch small airplanes take off and land.

3915 Clairmont Road   457-7236
Chamblee

Atlanta Braves Stadium

"Take me out to the ball game. Take me out to the park." This tour is sure to be a hit with any baseball fan. You'll get a tour of the stands, field, press box and all the "ins" and "outs" of the stadium.

Atlanta Braves Baseball Club   522-7630
521 Capitol Ave. S.E.
Atlanta

Capitol

See the seat of government for the state of Georgia. Learn a little about history as well as how much gold is on the dome. Tours begin at 10 and 11 a.m., 1 and 2 p.m. on weekdays. The Capitol is open Saturday, 10 a.m.–2 p.m. and Sunday, 1–3 p.m. but there are no guided tours available. No reservations required.

Capitol Hill and Washington St.   656-2844
Atlanta

Chattahoochee Water Treatment Plant

At the Chattahoochee Plant you'll see how water is collected and treated to make it safe to drink. This plant is capable of treating 40 million gallons of water a day!

2532 Bolton Road N.W.   355-7310
Atlanta

CNN Studio

This guided walking tour of Cable News Network and Headline News lets you witness the news coverage from news gathering to on-air presentation. Tours are given on the hour, Monday through Friday from 10 a.m. to 5 p.m. and weekends from 10 a.m. to 4 p.m. There is a $4 fee for adults and $2 for students.

1 CNN Center   827-2300
Marietta St. @ Techwood Drive
Atlanta

Coca-Cola Bottling Company

Watch the "real thing" fill up the bottles and cans at the Coca-Cola Bottling Plant in Marietta. The best part of the tour will be sampling the drink that made Atlanta famous. The plant is closed for construction until Spring 1991.

Old Highway 41   424-9080
Marietta

Fire Station

Preschoolers will be delighted with a tour of your local fire station. The tour will include the sleeping and eating quarters, equipment, and, of course, the fire truck. Each city and county has a different method for arranging tours, so call before you go.

Fox Theatre

The "Fabulous Fox," designated a National Landmark, features twinkling stars, moving clouds and an ornate Egyptian Ballroom. This tour helps you relive the grandeur of this 1920s theater. Admission is $3 for adults and $1 for children under 12. Tours are Monday, Thursday and Saturday at 10 a.m.

660 Peachtree St. N.E.   881-2100
Atlanta

Frito-Lay

Visit the home of the "bet you can't eat just one!" potato chip. You'll see how food is processed from a fresh potato, until it's washed, peeled, cooked, packaged and loaded on the truck. Tours are given every Thursday at 12:30, 2, 3:30 and 4:45 p.m.

4950 Peachtree Industrial Blvd.   455-6464 ext. 11
Chamblee

Georgia Department of Transportation

Watch the testing of materials used in making highways. Tours available Monday–Friday, 8 a.m.–4:45 p.m. Children must be 10 years old and older. Reservations required.

15 Kennedy Drive   363-7520
Forest Park

Governor's Mansion

The residence of the Governor of Georgia is located on 18 acres on West Paces Ferry. It is furnished with nineteenth century paintings, porcelains and an outstanding collection of Federal period furniture. The mansion is open Tuesday, Wednesday and Thursday from 10 to 11:30 a.m.

391 W. Paces Ferry Road N.W.   261-1776
Atlanta

Herndon House

Mansion built by Alonzo Herndon, founder of the second-largest black insurance company, Atlanta Life Insurance. Guided tours Tuesday–Saturday, 10 a.m.–4 p.m.

587 University Place   581-9813
Atlanta

Krispy Kreme

Krispy Kreme is a wonderland where thousands of doughnuts roll off conveyors day and night. Children can see how the dough is mixed, shaped, cooked, iced and packaged. Tours are given on Thursdays from 8:30–noon.

295 Ponce de Leon Ave. N.E.   876- 7307
Atlanta

Monastery of the Holy Spirit

You will get a feeling of peace when you visit this tranquil cloister built entirely by the Trappist brothers who live and work here. Tours focus on the history of the monastery, the Gothic abbey, beautiful grounds, greenhouse and bookstore. You'll also want to sample some of the delicious bread that is milled and baked on the premises.

Hwy. 212   483-8705
Conyers

Neely Nuclear Research Center

On the campus of Georgia Institute of Technology, families can see how nuclear energy is produced at a working reactor. Children should be older than third grade. Reservations required. Monday–Friday, 8 a.m.–5 p.m.; closed noon–1 p.m.

900 Atlantic Drive   894-3600
Atlanta

Newspapers

Many of your neighborhood newspapers open their doors to groups of children. These tours enable children to see what goes into the writing, printing and distribution of the weekly editions.

Atlanta Journal-Constitution

Their Gwinnett plant shows kids how a newspaper is printed. Reservations are required. Children must be 12 years or older.

6455 Best Friends Road   263-3963
Norcross

Marietta Daily

Tours are available Tuesday and Wednesday from 1–3 p.m. for groups of 8 and more. Children must be over 7. Reservations required.

580 Fairground St. S.E.   428-9411, ext. 218
Marietta

Police Station

A tour of the police department can be an exciting one for youngsters and their parents. Helicopters, motorcycles, the radio room and firing range are a few of the sights you will see.

DeKalb County Police Station   294-2564
4400 Memorial Drive
Tucker

Post Office

At the main post office on Crown Road, children can follow the route of the mail through automated equipment as it is sorted and canceled. You can also arrange tours of your local post office by calling it directly.

3900 Crown Road   765-7309
Hapeville

Power Plant

Jack McDonough is a coal-fired power plant, where workers will describe the motors, generators and pumps used to produce electricity. Georgia Power also offers tours at some of its other plants. Children must be 10 or older.

5551 S. Cobb Drive   433-7702
Smyrna

Restaurants

Flop it; pat it; fry it; freeze it. Squirt ketchup on it; throw pepperoni over it; put tartar sauce on it; sprinkle colored sugar on it. Anyway you slice it or serve it, children will be fascinated by tours of their favorite restaurants!

Captain D's
Carvel Ice Cream
Dunkin' Doughnuts
McDonald's
Pizza Hut
TCBY

Scottish Rite Children's Medical Center

A hospital tour is offered to children and their families at Scottish Rite Children's Medical Center. This tour, which includes a visit to the emergency room, an empty hospital room and other pediatric facilities, can take the fear out of hospital stays.

Scottish Rite Children's Medical Center   256-5252
1001 Johnson Ferry Road
Atlanta

Southface Energy Institute

Learn about the many types of energy including new alternate sources. The institute also promotes the wise use of energy and other natural resources. Monday–Friday, 9 a.m.–5 p.m.

158 Moreland Ave. S.E.   525-7657
Atlanta

State Farmer's Market

The Farmer's Market in Forest Park is the second largest produce market in the United States. Ride the "Fresh Express" tram over the market's 146 acres to see fresh produce, plants, the cannery and egg packing plant. Call in advance.

16 Forest Parkway   366-6910
Forest Park

Television Stations

Introduce children to the world of lights, cameras and show biz with a tour of one of Atlanta's television stations.

WAGA TV 5
1551 Briarcliff Road N.E.   875-5551
Atlanta

WXIA TV 11
1611 W. Peachtree St. N.E.   892-1611
Atlanta

WSB TV 2 and Radio AM 750 and FM 98.5
1601 W. Peachtree St. N.E.   897-7369
Atlanta

WPBA TV 30
740 Bismark Road N.E.   827-8900
Atlanta

Walking Tours

The Atlanta Preservation Center offers walking tours of six historic areas including: the Capitol area and Underground; historic downtown commercial center; the Fox Theatre district; the Inman Park residential area; Oakland Cemetery and Wren's Nest/West End. Tours are $3 donation for adults and $2 for students.

84 Peachtree St. N.W.   522-4345
Atlanta

TRIPS AND EXCURSIONS

Agrirama

I f you have a day, then pack up and get away to one of these sites around the state. One of the original 13 colonies, home flourishing Indian civilizations for hundreds of years and a major battleground of the Civil War, Georgia is steeped in history and covered with historic sites. Its natural beauty ranges from the mountains of the north where the Appalachian Trail begins, to the coastal islands of the south, where Cumberland Island National Seashore is one of the last, largely undisturbed barrier islands open to the public. Following are some places to explore within a few hours' drive of Atlanta. You'll see why you should "stay and see Georgia!"

Andersonville

Andersonville is a picturesque little town that was once the site of the infamous Confederate prison. The 475-acre national park and historic site now contains a national cemetery, Prisoner of War Museum and visitors center. There is a restored Pioneer Farm with a log cabin, grist mill and farm animals, as well as the Drummer Boy Civil War Museum, which contains a large collection of period artifacts.

I-75 South to GA 49   (912) 924-2558
Andersonville
Driving Time: 2½ hours

Athens

Athens, often referred to as the "Classic City," is the home of the University of Georgia. Athens is also home to many historic places and antebellum mansions. The Georgia Museum of Art is located on campus, and it features major traveling exhibitions, in addition to works from the permanent collection of 5,000 pieces. At the State Botanical Gardens of Georgia are cultivated gardens, five miles of hiking trails and a glass conservatory housing tropical plants.

East on U.S. 78   (404) 549-6800
Driving Time: 1½ hours

Babyland General

On the way to the north Georgia mountains, take time to visit Babyland General in Cleveland. "Doctors" and "nurses" put on a real show as they "deliver" Cabbage Patch Kids. Visitors can also "adopt" a doll and receive an official birth certificate with the doll.

I-85 North to I-985, then U.S. 129   (404)865-5505
19 Underwood Street
Cleveland
Driving Time; 1½ hours

Callaway Gardens

"Everything under the sun" is at Callaway Gardens just 90 miles south of Atlanta. There are scenic drives, nature trails and bike paths over the 2,500 acres of native flowers and woodlands. Recreational activities include golf, tennis, fishing, horseback riding and a beautiful sand beach with water-skiing shows. Also be sure to visit the John A. Sibley Horticultural Center, Cecil B. Day Butterfly Center, Ida Cason Callaway Memorial Chapel, and the Pioneer Log Cabin. Several restaurants and accommodations are also available.

I-85 South to I-185, then U.S. 27 to Pine Mountain   (404) 663-2281
Driving Time: 1½ hours

Chattanooga

On the way to Chattanooga, stop off at Chickamauga Battlefield, the nation's largest and oldest military park. There is a slide program about the battles fought here and a weapons collection, as well as more than 50 miles of hiking trails. When you get to Chattanooga, take an exciting ride on the Lookout Mountain Incline Railway. At Rock City you'll find beautiful flowers and trees, while children will be delighted with the Fairyland Caverns and Mother Goose Village. Ruby Falls, the Chattanooga Choo-Choo Complex, Chattanooga Nature Center, Tennessee Valley Railroad Museum Depot, a riverboat ride and lots more.

I-75 North   (616) 756-2121
Driving Time: 2 hours

Cloudland Canyon

On the western edge of Lookout Mountain is Cloudland Canyon State Park, offering scenic vistas of the ridges and valleys of Northwest Georgia. The park straddles a deep gorge, with some waterfalls almost 100 feet high.

I-75 North to Ga. 136, Lafayette   (404) 657-4050
Driving Time: 2½ hours

Dahlonega

"There's gold in them thar hills" as you will discover when you visit Dahlonega. The restored town with its antique and arts and crafts shops looks much as it did when it was a boom town for the gold rush in the 1830s. At the Gold Museum on the square you can view the history of mining, along with an exhibit of gold coins and nuggets, and you can take the kids to pan for gold and other gemstones in the area.

Ga. 400 North   (404) 864-2257
Driving Time: 1 hour

Etowah Indian Mounds

This is the site of a prehistoric Indian settlement that was occupied from A.D. 700 to 1650. Pottery, axes, bones and other artifacts in the museum give insight into the lives of Indians who hunted and cultivated crops in this valley hundreds of years ago. See the film "The Early Americans," then walk to the mounds. A nature trail leads to the Etowah River, where you can enjoy a picnic. Just to the north of Cartersville, at U.S. 411, is William Weinman Mineral Museum with a cave formation, extensive Georgian specimens, touch-and-feel exhibits and an outstanding mineral collection.

I-75 North to Ga. 113 and 61, Cartersville   (404) 382-2704
Driving Time: 1 hour

Fort Mountain State Park

Fort Mountain is a perfect place to go camping or to go for a picnic. Explore the ancient rock wall to the top of the mountain, enjoy the panoramic view from the lookout tower, hike the nature trails, or go for a swim. Near Fort Mountain in Spring Place is the brick mansion of Cherokee Chief James Vann, which was built in 1804.

I-75 North fo Ga. 52, Chatsworth   (404) 695-2621
Driving Time: 1½ hours

Helen

Would you like to visit a charming Bavarian Alpine Village with window boxes, gingerbread houses and cobblestone streets? Then come to Helen. You'll find shops with cheese, candy, toys, Christmas decorations and baked treats. And each fall there is dancing and merry entertainment to the omm-pah bands at the Oktoberfest.

A few miles up the road from Helen is Unicoi State Park. You can enjoy camping, swimming, nature trails, or spectacular Anna Ruby Falls. Also worth a visit is Brasstown Bald, the state's highest mountain.

Ga. 400 North to Ga. 17-75   (404) 878-2181
Driving Time: 1 ½ hours

Macon

Macon is a major center of historical, architectural and cultural attractions. You can visit the birthplace of poet Sidney Lanier, tour the famous 24-room Hay House mansion, explore the Macon Museum of Arts and Sciences, or take in the Harriet Tubman Historical and Cultural Museum. A special time to visit Macon is during the Cherry Blossom Festival at the end of March.

Near Macon is the Ocmulgee National Monument, which features Indian mounds, exhibits of six distinct Indian groups, and a ceremonial council chamber. Native American arts and crafts demonstrations are held throughout the year.

Also close to Macon is the Jarrell Plantation in Juliette. This working farm complex, which spans 100 years, features animals, crops, a steam-powered mill and blacksmith shop.

I-75 South   (912) 743-3401
Driving Time: 1 ½ hours

Milledgeville

Georgia's capital for 60 years, Milledgeville is home to many antebellum structures, including the old Governor's Mansion, the old State Capitol Building and Saint Stephen's Episcopal Church, used to stable Union horses during the Civil War. A two-hour trolley tour winds through the historic district. Part of the Antebellum Trail, Milledgeville is reached by way of Eatonton, home of the Uncle Remus Museum. Each year Milledgeville is the site of the Brown's Crossing Craftsman Fair in October and April.

I-20 East to Ga. 441 South   (912) 452-4687
Driving Time: 1 ½ hours

New Echota State Historic Site

New Echota was once the capital of the Cherokee Nation and home of Sequoyah, inventor of the Cherokee alphabet. The settlement consisted of houses, stores, a ferry, school, courthouse, council house, mission station, and even a print shop where the bilingual newspaper, "The Phoenix," was produced. The museum provides a look at the Cherokee's rich culture before they were forced westward on the "Trail of Tears."

I-75 North to Ga. 225, Calhoun   (404) 629-8151
Driving Time: 1 ½ hours

Tifton

The Agrirama is a living history village of rural Georgia in the 1800s. There are more than 35 authentic restorations including a gristmill, cotton gin, turpentine still and logging train. Interpreters are available to demonstrate lifestyles and trades of a hundred years ago from soap-making to spinning and plowing.

I-75 South, Tifton   (912) 386-3344
Driving Time: 3½ hours

Warm Springs

After Franklin Delano Roosevelt was crippled by polio in 1921, he went to Warm Springs for therapy and fell in love with the springs and the village. On a visit to the Little White House Museum, you can see the president's home, car, wheelchairs, a film and other memorabilia. Little has changed since he died there in 1945.

Near the Little White House is the restored village of Warm Springs and F. D. Roosevelt State Park, where you can hike, camp, or go for a swim in the rock swimming pool that is shaped like the Liberty Bell.

I-85 South to U.S. 27A   (404) 655-3511
Driving Time: 1 ½ hours

Westville

Westville

Westville is a functioning living history village "where it's always 1850." There are more than 30 historic buildings, as well as costumed craftsmen who demonstrate weaving, pottery-making, blacksmithing, cobbling, quilting, syrup-making and leather-working. Nearby is Georgia's "Little Grand Canyon" in Providence Canyon State Park.

I-85 South to I-185, then U.S. 27 to Lumpkin   Westville (912) 838-5310
Driving Time: 2½ hours   Providence (912) 838-6202

Take this opportunity to subscribe to Atlanta's most informative parenting newspaper, Atlanta Parent

- Atlanta's most comprehensive family calendar
- Timely parenting articles with ideas and tips for raising your family in the 90s
- Regular columns include "Discover Atlanta," "Pack Up & Go," "Atlanta Parent Talks With" and more!

To subscribe send $12 for one year to:

Atlanta Parent
P. O. Box 8506
Atlanta, GA 30306

Name _____

Address _____

City _____ State _____ Zip _____

Phone _____

ABOUT THE AUTHORS

Kids' Atlanta was written by two Atlanta residents who know the ins and outs of this wonderful city. The authors know first-hand about Atlanta's offerings for children.

Liz White is publisher of Atlanta Parent newspaper, a monthly parenting publication that has served Atlanta families since 1983. A 15-year resident of Atlanta, she and her husband Mark, realized the need for localized parenting information after the birth of their daughter Laura. Their research assistant is now nine years old.

Jean Feldman, Ph.D. is an Atlanta native and an early childhood specialist. She has more than 20 years experience in education and is a frequent presenter to community and professional groups as well as the author of several early childhood education books. Jean and her husband John, are the parents of two teenagers, Holly and Nick.

Future Editions

If your facility, program, business or organization was not included in
KIDS' ATLANTA, complete this form so you can be included in future editions.

Name of Program, Organization or Business _____

_____

Description _____

_____

_____

_____

Address _____
                                      Street

_____
                City   State   Zip

Phone _____

Hours _____

Cost _____

Additional Information _____

Contact Person _____

Mail to: ATLANTA PARENT
              P. O. Box 8506
              Atlanta, GA 30306

NOTES

NOTES

NOTES

NOTES